Little Boy Big World

Little Boy Big World

Hayatullah H. Rahmatullah

LITTLE BOY BIG WORLD

Published in the United States of America.

Copyright © 2017 by Hayatullah H. Rahmatullah

All rights reserved. No part of this publication may be reproduced, distributed, or transmitted in any form or by any means, including photocopying, recording, or electronic or mechanical methods, without the prior written permission of the author.

ISBN-13: 978-0-9990846-0-1

Edited by Stephanie J. Beavers Communications

Cover design by Arian Hashemi

Dedication

This book is dedicated to my father, my Baba. He is a good man who taught me much about life and family.

Editor's Preface

I worked with Hayat for a number of months to bring his book to fruition. Given that he was born and raised in Afghanistan, and now lives and works most months of the year in Dubai, ours has necessarily been a long distance relationship, one founded by a Facebook referral from a friend of a friend. (The second friend mentioned here is Leslie, who appears later in Hayat's story.)

The more I delved into Hayat's story, the more I felt for him and his family, given what they have had to endure over the years—although I am quite certain that neither Hayat nor his family want or expect pity. Some occurrences described in the book are horrific, and no human should ever have to experience them. Other day-to-day lifestyle, traditions, and mores, though seemingly hard or objectionable or backwards (pick your adjective) when compared to those of other cultures (especially Western), are accepted by the Afghani people without question and, frankly, without complaint.

This story covers Hayat's life from adolescence (age 9) to present day (age 25), and is told through his own eyes and in his own words. He wrote his story during Ramadan 2015 and used the help of: 1) mobile technology and 2) Leslie, who cut and pasted his words from text messages into a Word document. In one of my initial email exchanges with Leslie, she said, "He wrote with great passion. Parts were difficult emotionally to write."

With his words now on paper, Hayat needed advice, guidance, and professional help to bring the story to life. One editor, Susan, started the project. Eventually the work transitioned to me. Admittedly, I was, at first, hesitant. After all, how could I possibly work with a client whose English was elementary at best, not to mention who lived in a time zone nine hours ahead of my own? How would I ever get paid for my work? Thanks to Leslie's kind words—and Hayat's dogged persistence—I accepted the job. I should note that Leslie and I both attended the same college, and with that associated connection, I could not possibly say no. I am so glad I did not. I see now how petty my initial concerns were.

Hayat and I exchanged email communications throughout the project every three or four days. Toward the end, Hayat and I spoke by phone to go over a few final edits. His written English, though comprehensible in most instances, was difficult to follow in others. When you add in cultural distinctions requiring clarification, the 12+ months to complete the project were not unreasonable. Hayat's passion did not wane during the entire process. If anything, it grew stronger, the closer we got to the finish line.

I hope readers enjoy this book. You will meet a youthful, playful Hayat, who loves to learn and who knows enough to ask all the right questions. You will see an inquisitive, fun Hayat, who loves life, his family, and his lifelong friend Juma with all his heart. Lastly, you will see a Hayat whose innocence is abruptly stolen from him and who is expected to grow up—while still a boy—to support his family business. Whatever vision and opinion you currently possess of your own life is bound to change for the good after reading this book.

Stephanie J. Beavers, Editor

Acknowledgements

I would like to thank, first and foremost, Leslie Putnam Orr, for her friendship, kindness, and support. Without her help, I would never have been able to complete this book.

I would like to thank Stephanie Beavers for editing my book and working with me over many months to prepare my book for publishing

Chapter One
2000

Today is January 1, 2000. Snow fell as I slept last night, covering our province for the first time this winter. My home is in Paktika Province, in the Sarobi District, Neway Pasany. You probably would just call it Afghanistan.

It is early morning, the sky is clean and blue, washed thoroughly with the new day's light. The snow, in its attempt to mirror the heavens, sparkles brightly enough to blind me. I'm the first one out, running through the snow that surrounds my home. It's so bright! I want my sisters to join me, to help me build a snowman. I want to share this moment with them. It is so beautiful and white and fresh and cold. How can I explain how great it is when there is new snow on a new day?

Finally, the three girls emerge from the hall of our home, one at a time. First comes Sobia, the oldest. Being older than me, Sobia often tells me what to do, whether I like it or not. Next is Shakila, the middle one, who was everyone's favorite until Nadia was born. Then I came along... not just the youngest... but a boy! I am very lucky. Not that I get all the favors, but I *am* a boy, and I *am* the youngest. Who *wouldn't* want to shower me with gifts? My fortune came early on, as my parents were given a goat and a huge milk cow when I was born—to help me become strong. Despite the fact that I avoid milk because it upsets my stomach, the knowledge of these gifts strengthened my will and warmed me.

I call out to my sisters, "It's time for our snowman to come to life." They run toward me, all smiles, their breath visible in the crisp air. The freshness of the morning's air and the beautiful snow excite us all, and we direct this energy into building a snowman. He is magnificent. We use three big balls of the packed white snow to build him. Well, if I'm being honest, we use two big balls for his body and stack a little one on top for his head. One of my sisters gets three pieces of burnt, spent wood from my mother's bread oven to use for our snowman's eyes and nose—the contrast of black on white creates his expression. Compared to the rotund American snowmen I've seen in pictures, this one is a bit lacking. But he is our snowman. Our shared sense of pride is unspoken, but I feel it. He is our snowman, and he is strong, and it is the first snow. The day cannot be any more perfect.

My sisters have come out in their warm coats and their hijabs, so their insides are warm. But they wear no gloves and, despite the perfection of this moment, their hands have turned painfully cold and red as a result of our snow creation. For me, the youngest, I am happy and excited and just alive, like a bird flitting through the season's first snow. The girls, however, are mad at me because the idea to build the snowman was mine and they did it barehanded. I just laugh at them. How can you be mad when you form a man from winter's first gift?

Before I decide to care that my sisters are upset, I hear our mom calling us for breakfast. I love breakfast. Our food is prepared in our family home, and I think the smells and sounds of this are just perfection. Everyone in the family has a job to do—my mom's job is to take care of meals. She bakes fresh, flat bread for every meal. She places the dough inside the oven, and the dough tells you when it's ready by first getting big, and then small. I love my mother's bread, and the delicious smell of the bread cooking in the oven inside our home. Besides the first day of snow, there is nothing better than my mom's cooking. Actually, her food is better than fresh snow, for it provides me with warmth, while snow is cold, yet they are both an intrinsic part of our home.

My sisters and I come in out of the winter to eat breakfast with our family. Grandparents, uncles, aunts, cousins, sisters... This is my family, and these are the people I live with. I can't remember a time when we did not all eat together—well, that is, before Dubai happened. Dubai, a city in the United Arab Emirates (UAE), changed everything. But the events of my story occur before Dubai, so this morning we are eating together. It is cold outside and breakfast is good. Just as I do every day, I have eggs, hot bread, and tea to warm me. (I don't really drink milk—even if the goat it comes from was a gift.)

Now I must explain why the first snow in my village is special. It is not because we can build a snowman, but because after the first snowfall occurs, we can write a *burfi*—a special letter that gets delivered to a neighbor. If, after the first snow, you are the first to deliver a burfi to your neighbor and get him to read it, you get a dinner for your entire family!

You can give the burfi to any member of a neighboring family, but you must be quick and give the burfi before one is given to you. If you are first, you and your family win, and then your neighbor must host your entire family for a most delicious dinner. If your neighbor is a rich man, he must sacrifice a goat for this meal. If he is not rich, he can cook anything, as long as the meal includes meat. Many people in Afghanistan cannot read or write, yet we all know what a burfi is.

Keeping in mind that it is the first snow, I quickly finish my breakfast and ask Baba to write the burfi.

"What do you want it to say?" asks Baba. He is smiling.

"You have to cook dinner for our entire family and we choose our dinner," I respond. Baba agrees and begins to write the burfi as I hurriedly prepare for the cold outside.

Not a single minute later, Baba and I leave to take the burfi—my simple message—to our closest neighbor. The message states, "Catch me before I get to the mosque." If they don't catch me, they cook us dinner. But if they do catch me, then we must cook them dinner. It is a race, and I will need to be quick to win. Luckily, I am. My neighbor's house isn't too far from ours, and it is directly on the road to the *masjid*—the mosque. Good planning, right?

Baba hides behind a tree on the side of the road as I go up to the door. If my neighbor sees Baba, they will know something is up, maybe even that there is a burfi. So we know we need to surprise them.

I knock on the door, readying myself to run. The father of the house opens the door and invites me in for breakfast, which is the honorable thing to do when someone visits your house.

I am quick with my response. "No, thank you. I just came to give you this!" Everyone looks at my hands to see what I bring this early in the morning. As fast as I can, I throw the burfi inside, and take off running toward the mosque.

I hear my father laugh as our neighbor chases me down the road. It does not matter that it is cold or that there is snow on the ground. I run like the headwinds of a storm. Our fat neighbor cannot catch me, and I reach the mosque safely, breathless in the cold air. I turn around to see my pursuer far behind on the road. Baba strides proudly behind him, smiling. We won.

We will go to their home that night and they will serve us dinner. I know we will have Kabuli rice with carrots and raisins—and meat, of course! The food my mother makes is, without doubt, the best. But this night's meal will be a prize, and prizes taste amazing. Besides, seeing my mother enjoy a meal that she didn't have to cook makes this prize that much more extraordinary and special.

The day gets even better when, as we return home, my father shares with me that I will soon be starting school. Once winter is over, school will begin, and I will be there when it starts. I've seen the exterior of the school house but have never been inside. I wonder what happens in school. Maybe I will meet some friends. Friends to race and build snowmen with, friends that won't get mad because their hands freeze in the snow.

* * *

The snow is long gone and, along with the warmer weather, comes the day for school to start. School usually begins in April and lasts for two and a half months, after which we have exams. School break in the winter lasts three months! I have never been to school before and, at the age of nine, I am very excited for this, as I am the first boy from my entire family to seek a formal education. I have one notebook and one pen for this new adventure—a trip that will take me to the small schoolhouse in the village. The school has eight rooms and two teachers.

Baba accompanies me on the fifteen-minute walk to school. He looks at me as I carry my notebook and pen in my hand, and seems to know what I am thinking. He says, "Hayat, today you will go to school without a school bag. I will buy one for you that you can start using tomorrow." This further lifts my spirits, and I just about run the rest of the way to school.

In school, once all the other students have arrived, the teacher looks at me and asks, "Are you new to the class?"

I say, "I'm new to the school," and all the students laugh at me even though I did not say anything wrong. I ignore them all as the teacher silences them.

After the class has settled, he then says, "I am Naseeb Khan, your teacher, and I am *not* new to this school. I have been responsible for many, many children, so trust me when I tell you that I have seen it all."

My first lesson is Pashto, our language, the language of the Pashtuns, and one of two official languages of Afghanistan. The teacher explains that we will learn to read, write, and properly speak our language. Thus, I begin my studies.

At 11:30, before the sun gets too high in the sky, we finish school and I head back home alone. I am thinking about the events of the morning, and how this walk home seems much longer than the trip to school earlier with Baba. Suddenly, I hear someone running up behind me. I turn and see it is one of the boys from my class.

"What is your name?" the boy asks.

"Hayat," I reply. "What is your name?"

"Juma."

"Juma," I repeat. "Are you new at school too?"

"Yes. This is my first day," he says, with a proud smile.

I wonder why none of the other students laughed at him that day, yet they all laughed at me, on my first day of school. But, no matter, for Juma is my very first friend, and here we are—walking, laughing, and talking together. We can only walk together for a short time since we live on different sides of the village, about fifteen minutes apart. But this is much better than making the long walk home completely alone. Eventually the road splits, and he has to take his way and I take mine. We say our goodbyes for the day, and each continue on toward our respective homes. That split in the road took us both to many different places. It still does.

When I get home, Mom is waiting for me at the door, ready to welcome me back into the nest with a hug. But school has drained me and I am very hungry. I really have no time for a hug! I wriggle from her arms and run right past her into the kitchen. At lunch, everyone is happy for me, especially Sobia, my oldest sister, who is very smart. She has never had the opportunity to go to school, but some people are smart without having attended school. And that is Sobia, although I can see through her smiles and know that she would also like to go to school.

Lunch is so filling, and school was so exhausting, that once we finish eating, I plan to rest a bit. I crave a nap, but Baba comes home before I am able to fall asleep. He has gone all the way to the Sarobi District to buy me a new bag for school—just as he had promised that morning! We can't buy these bags in any of the three shops in my village because those shops sell just the basics, the things people need on a day-to-day basis. But school bags are something special. When I see it, I am so happy I forget about sleeping. I just can't leave my bag alone, snapping and unsnapping the pockets, zipping and unzipping the main compartment, seeing exactly how many books and papers and pencils and pens it can hold. I would take the bag with me for my rest, but now I am so excited about my new bag that I am no longer sleepy.

I decide to go out to the village and show my bag to my new friend Juma. Sobia sees me leaving and says, "Hayat, school is closed for the day. Where are you going with your school bag?"

"I am going to show my friend my school bag," I respond, certain that the mention of my new friend will make my sister curious.

She doesn't question what I have just said, but instead simply tells me to be home by dinner.

I went to the address where Juma told me he lives, and am happy when he opens the door. I show him my brand new school bag, but soon realize I am not as happy as I thought I would be. You ask why? Because, although Juma likes my bag, he immediately tells me he wants one just like it! He is going to ask his father to buy him the same bag as mine. I really don't like this idea.

"Why do you want the same bag?" I question him. "Surely the other students will laugh at both of us if we go to school tomorrow with the same bag!"

"It is simple," Juma states, "because we are friends!"

As I think about what he has said, it all makes perfect sense. You see, I realize that he *is* my friend, and so he *should* have the same bag. "Okay, Juma," I say, "I will ask my Baba where he got my bag."

Even as grown men with our businesses in the Naif Souq shopping center in Old Dubai, so far away from our own country, I still think back to that moment in our childhood. Today, when Juma says he is going to buy a mobile phone exactly like my own new mobile phone, I still get mad at him. And then he asks me to show him how to use it! To think that we didn't even have land lines back home in Afghanistan, and here we are in 2015 with modern technology.

Another thing we didn't have in Afghanistan is playgrounds. I did not know what a playground was until I heard the word from a soldier and he showed me a picture of an American playground. I know one thing, the Taliban for sure would never build us playgrounds. If it is not something they want, they won't build it. But we have a jungle all around my village. That is our playground—one that does not have to be built by the Taliban. The jungle gives us animals and plants and things to climb—we will never tire of it.

Once Juma and I have settled the issue of the school bag, I look out the window and see a yellow bird sitting in a tree. I say, "Hey, Juma, let's follow that yellow bird." Juma worries the bird will fly away, but I tell him, "Come on. Let's try. Let's go find the bird's nest." Out the door we go. Most birds in Afghanistan build their nests deep inside the jungle, but that day we are lucky, as we see that the bird flies around to the other side of the tree where there is a hole.

Juma runs to the trunk and looks up the tall tree. "The nest is in there—I know it," he says.

I look up and see the nest-hole is high up. We can't climb the tree so I tell Juma, "Let's go for now. We know where the nest is and can come back some other time to check it out."

The rumble in my stomach tells me it is dinner time, and time for us both to go home. We are excited for tomorrow's lessons, because even as young boys, we understand that not everyone gets to go to school. My sisters don't get to go, and they never will. I am also excited because I know that not everyone gets an amazing book bag for school, not even my best friend Juma—at least not yet. I am still full of good luck.

Despite all the excitement of the day, I have no trouble falling asleep that night. I clench my school bag close to my chest. The next morning, I feel fully refreshed. As soon as I finish breakfast, I get on my way for the fifteen-minute walk to school. This time I arrive at the same time as the other students. I carry my new book bag proudly, for all to see. Juma is late this day, however, and I have no idea why, which makes me nervous for him.

That day's lessons are on Islam. Everyone I have ever met is Muslim, and we honor Islam by learning from the Qur'an, the unaltered and final revelation of God. Our lessons will teach us how to pray and how to go to the masjid. Halfway through our class, Juma appears and Naseeb Khan yells at him for being tardy. Juma, respectful of the teacher, sits next to me without saying a word. We both look at our books and do not raise our eyes. Eventually, Naseeb resumes reading in his loud voice and we repeat after him.

After we finish our lessons, the teacher calls me to his office. Juma comes with me, even though I was told to go alone. He agrees to wait for me outside, and I enter our teacher's office.

"Please, Hayat, take a seat," Naseeb tells me. "Look, son, you seem to be a smart boy. You should keep your mind and your focus on studying, because you are the future of Afghanistan."

I laugh and say, "I am a small boy in a big world. How can I be the future of my country?"

My teacher is not pleased at my reaction. He does not see any humor in what he had just told me, and is angry that I am laughing. Seeing how I upset him, I want to apologize. But because I feel nervous and unsure of what to say, I say nothing. Naseeb Khan places his hand on top of my head and says, "Look at me. I call you *son* because I see something inside of you—something special."

I feel truth in what he is saying. His words lodge in my heart and brain, and I recall their powerful impact many times over in the years that follow. Feeling a need to say something, I blurt out, "Okay, but can I call you *sir* because I already have a Baba?"

He smiles and says, "Yes. Sir is fine."

Naseeb Khan is a good man and a caring teacher. Years later, on a trip back home from Dubai, I visited Naseeb Khan. He had only one leg. But this is now, and he dismisses me from his office. "Go now, home." On my way out the door he hands me a chocolate.

I find Juma, who is still waiting for me in the hallway. Even today, so many years later, I find myself with Juma at Naif Souq (Dubai's famous shopping center) and he still waits for me. I tell him that our teacher has given me a chocolate, and we share this sweet treat together. We leave school and start our return walk home, just as we had done the day before. But that day, before our paths diverge, I remember that I have five rupees.

"Juma, let's go to the shop and share something more to eat," I say.

Of the three small shops in our village, I choose the one with the best cakes. It turns out that the cakes here are three rupees each, so I realize I will need to convince the shopkeeper to give us two cakes for my five rupees. I wonder if I can do this.

"Sir," I say, "my friend and I have just finished school for the day. We have spent all morning learning, and are now in search of a treat." This gets a smile from the old man in the shop.

"Of course. Young boys like you are always working up tremendous appetites," he says. "How can I help you?"

"We would each like a cake, but have only five rupees to spend, and—"

"That is not a problem," he interrupts, "as long as you can return tomorrow and pay me one more rupee."

I tell him in complete honesty, "I am sorry, sir, but no. I won't have one more rupee tomorrow. I cannot make a promise that I know I will not be able to keep. The best I can do is give you five rupees for two cakes today."

He looks first at me, then at Juma, and says, "Fine, boys. Which cakes would you like?"

We each select a cake, thank the man, and get back on our way home. Juma is amazed that I could speak up to the man so earnestly. I am pleased with the deal I negotiated, but I tell Juma that I have much practice with my older sisters. As we arrive at the fork in the road, we make plans for after lunch. "Don't forget. We have to investigate the bird's nest. I will meet you back at your house, Juma."

Continuing along my way home, my mind wanders to my mother's cooking, and the lunch that awaits. Having never been to school, I hadn't realized that learning would create such an appetite. As I approach home, I see Mom is once again waiting for me at the door. This time, before she asks me anything, I ask her, "What did you cook for me?" She tells me that she has cooked vegetables and rice. I thank her and run past her into the house. I love vegetables!

At lunch I tell my family about everything I did at school and how kindly the teacher had spoken to me.

Mom is very proud of me. "This is so good, Hayat! You must become a doctor," she says.

Baba furls his thick eyebrows as he looks at me and says, "No. You shall become a businessman, making trips around the world, dealing with the most important people." You see, Baba has a shop in Dubai, in the United Arab Emirates. For him to be working away from home in another country is normal for him. His father did the same thing in India, and so did his father's father.

I don't really pay attention to what everyone is saying, and no one bothers to ask me what I want to be. They are all talking over each other, but I don't mind, because I am eating. They can keep talking all afternoon if they like, as long as I can keep eating this most delicious cooking. I also want to get through my lunch because I know that afterwards, I'll be going to Juma's house to look for the bird's nest. But first, I am so hungry that I have two full bowls of rice with vegetables, along with a piece of Mom's bread, and I savor every bite of it. I wash it all down with tea, and am soon ready to go back out, to return to Juma and the bird's nest. I tell Baba where I am going, and burst out the door.

I will be at Juma's house on the other side of the village in ten minutes—the time it takes to cross to the other side. As I walk along, I think about the size of my village. I have heard there are some six hundred homes here. Soon enough, I arrive at my friend's house and the first order of business is to find rope to help us climb the tree. We avoid telling his mom what we are looking for, because she might try to discourage us. When we finally find a length of rope, Juma and I tiptoe through the house so that she does not see us.

We approach the tree quietly this time, so as not to disturb the birds, and stop a moment to think about how to climb the tree without making too much noise. I throw the rope up, and after only two tries, loop it around a branch.

Juma does not want to climb, so I will be the one to shimmy up the rope, with him holding the bottom of it. I reach the hole where the nest is, and discover I have a problem—snakes. Snakes often live in trees, and I am afraid to put my hand in the hole. The story of my uncle being bit by a snake while picking fruit is in the forefront of my mind. I cannot let this slow me down, and I remind myself of the prize we are after—the nest. I hope for some luck and reach blindly into the nest hole. I first feel the twiggy roughness of the nest, and then, in the nest itself, three smooth, warm eggs. I call down, "Juma, there are eggs!"

"Leave them be, Hayat. We will let some days pass so that the eggs can hatch and become birds." I agree with him and climb back down the rope. We are both very happy at this discovery and look forward to having the birds. We may not have a playground, but where else could you climb a tree to see baby birds, if not in our jungle!

* * *

Four days later we return to the bird's nest. We once again sneak the rope out of Juma's house and sling it up the tree for me to climb. Something is making quite a lot of noise as I approach the nest, but this time I do not think it is snakes. When I feel inside the hole, I feel three baby birds!

"Juma, there are three baby birds in the nest," I yell down to my friend, "Three birds!"

"We can feed them good food in our homes, Hayat! Those baby birds will grow to be big and strong if we keep them in the safety of our homes," Juma says.

I decide this makes sense, and put two of the babies into my pockets. I leave one in the nest because the mother bird is very angry—she can't stop yelling at me and Juma. We don't care about her, however, because we know we are taking the baby birds to a safe place and will feed them better than if they stay in the jungle.

Of course, when I bring my bird home, Mom becomes like the big mom bird in the tree. She sees me holding the baby bird and becomes oh-so-very mad at me.

"You must take that bird back, Hayat! This is no jungle. We do not live in a nest like the little bird needs, and you most certainly cannot teach it how to fly!"

I plead. "But, Mom, I will keep it safe and give it good food—I will save some of what I do not eat and give it to the bird. Your food is much better than anything its mother could bring it. Besides, here with me it will not have to worry about snakes."

"Hayat, come here and listen to me, please. What if someone kidnapped you from me and Baba? How do you think we would we feel?"

Well, that gets me thinking. Even if the kidnappers fed me wonderfully and kept me in a safe place, I would never see Mom or Baba or my sisters again. I realize I am wrong to have taken the baby bird, and I decide to take it back to its nest—and its mother. I go straight to Juma's house with the bird cradled in my dirty hands. When I see Juma, I see that he is in the same situation with his own parents.

They are in the middle of explaining to him why he must take the bird back to the nest, and I interject and tell him that my parents don't want me to keep the bird either. Back we go to the jungle, where I climb the rope to the nest hole and return the two baby birds to their nest. I know it is the right thing to do, even if I want to keep them. I wanted to feed them, and help them grow big, watch their feathers come out and be ready to fly. I really do understand, however, that it is not my place to take them from their family.

On our way home, we see the Taliban approaching us in a white car. My father warned me about them, and told me what to look for in order to avoid them. These men in the car have long, long beards and hair, just as Baba said they would. They stop their car in front of us and lower a window.

"Where are you boys going?" asks one from inside the car.

"We are going home," I say. Even with that brief exchange, we feel their hatred for us just in how they are looking at us.

"May we continue on?" asks Juma, timidly. They don't reply, but just watch us, so I start walking. Their continued silence means they have allowed us to move along home. At this, our day has been ruined. We walk the rest of the way in silence, breaking it only to say goodbye.

I return home, exhausted. After dinner, I go to the room I share with my sisters and lie down on my floor mat where I go right to sleep. This night, even in my slumber, I sense the exact moment when each sister joins me in the room.

* * *

The next day, as I walk alone to school, I see from afar the same white Taliban car next to our small school building. I keep walking, warily, and when I reach my school, I see a terrifying scene. The Taliban are beating students who have long hair. They have scissors and are cutting every student's hair. Several students try to run away, but they don't get far, as the Taliban quickly catch them and beat them with a wire. No one speaks a word as the Taliban continue shearing hair. Our teacher does not try to stop them, for he knows he will be assassinated there, in front of the children. There is no middle ground or negotiating. Juma and I watch in silence, and pray for the lives of our school mates. In the end, we are spared, perhaps because we are only nine and our hair is not long enough to be worth cutting.

It is 11:30, and I am still outside my school. The Taliban are now ordering every student to not shave their beard and to always cut their hair short. I look at them and wonder why they don't cut their own hair. Their hair is long, so why must ours be short? I don't dare ask, however, for the wire beatings have left some students barely able to stand on their own. We know we must bow to the Taliban, or our own life, or that of our family, ends.

And now, our school day has been stolen by the Taliban. Many of the students were badly beaten. When the Taliban is finished, we all leave and return home like beaten dogs. Our sadness weighs us down and we are all crying.

When I arrive home, I tell my family about what the Taliban did that day at school. There is no avoiding what has happened, as much as I want to forget about this whole day. My mom, like so many others that day, cries, but she also seeks vengeance and asks Allah to destroy the Taliban government.

I am but a little boy who has only recently started school, but I know that no one wants the Taliban government. They have locations throughout every district in Afghanistan, and on days such as this, make trips to the villages to show how strong they are and to frighten the villagers. We are forced to accept what they do, as no other option exists.

In my own small world, I do not believe I was oblivious to the Taliban. I knew they existed and I knew enough to respect them out of fear of harm to me or my family more than anything. But that day, I wanted to forget about the Taliban and simply go out and play with Juma. In the jungle, Juma and I are able to be boys. We check on the bird's nest and play hide-and-seek for hours, until it is time to go back home and get ready for school the next day. To this very day, however, whenever I see a white car like the one the Taliban used to drive, the horrifying memories of their evil deeds return to haunt me.

* * *

After five months, we reach the end of the school year. I am thankful the Taliban have not come back to our school. Tomorrow I have final exams. I have worked very hard to be ranked first or second in my class. Deep into the night I study, reading through each book and trying to make sense of the writing in my notebook. Being in first position would make Baba and Mom very proud of me, and justify their decision to send me to school. I know I cannot stay awake all night long so, after reading through every one of my school books, I do my best to fall asleep in the crowded room I share with my sisters.

Morning comes quickly, and by 7:30 I am up and dressed for school. Mom prepares me a special breakfast and tells me she is sure I will be the top-ranked student in my class. I hope to make her proud. After breakfast, I walk the fifteen minutes to school. I arrive just in time, as Naseeb Khan is telling everyone to get ready for the exam. He hands each student a copy of the exam, and I feel confident as I am able to work through every question.

I know I must do well on the exam, but I get excited at the thought of the summer vacation that awaits me as soon as I finish! When I am done, I wait for Juma to complete his exam. He finally finishes, which means our summer has begun! Juma and I walk home together. Along the way, we plan what we will do for the next three months. That day, however, I take Juma to my house for lunch, and then we will play on my family's farm. Our farm has some one hundred apple trees to explore and climb.

Mom serves us our lunch, and we eat happily as we continue to plan our three-month vacation. Then everything changes. Like that, our happy mood disappears as, over the loudspeakers that blare out from the mosque across the village, we hear the voice of a Taliban soldier. He booms out that all students must report to the mosque. Juma and I practically drop our bowls of food for fear of what will happen if we are late. When we arrive at the mosque, we see all the students from school along with Naseeb Khan and another teacher.

The Taliban tell us that each one of us must report to the Sarobi District every morning at nine o'clock. At first, nobody dares ask why—this is how it works with them. However, my teacher is the only one brave enough to ask one of the Taliban leaders why the children must do this. I am sad when I hear the answer. The Taliban man says they are going to be building new rooms and they are requesting our help. Of course, we know they aren't *requesting* our help—we have no a choice in the matter. We are one hundred and fifty students who will serve as free summer labor for the Taliban. We will work for no pay, and the Taliban will have their new rooms. This is reinforced when they tell us the penalty of missing one day: a three-day stay in jail without food.

The Taliban collects a list of names of all the students from our teacher. I'm very sad at this moment—not only for myself, but for everyone else who is forced to do these kinds of things for the Taliban. I look around and see everyone else is just as sad. You see, we have no choice in this. We have to do what they tell us. They have the power to force us. If we do not go to the Sarobi District, the Taliban will beat us and keep us in jail without feeding us.

The Taliban dismisses us and everyone returns home for the rest of the day, where we tell our families the bad news. I once again make my mom cry with my story of the Taliban, only this time she wails and curses for Allah to destroy the Taliban government. Only Allah—no one else—can save us from the Taliban.

My hopes and plans for summer vacation have been dashed. I know that tomorrow is a big day—my first working for the Taliban—so I decide to go to sleep.

The next morning, all the students are at our designated meeting place on time. All day, we must haul stone, wood, and any other materials they need to build their dormitories. They feed us a small lunch and provide us water when we need it. After a few days of this work Juma gets sick and is unable to go to work with us. He asks me to tell the Taliban that he is sick, and I reluctantly agree.

When I get to work, I report to the Taliban that Juma is sick, but that he will be at work the next day. When the Taliban leader hears that news, he slaps me. "Today your friend Juma is sick! Tomorrow, someone else will say the same thing and there will be no one to build the rooms!"

I hear them tell their driver to go back to the village and bring the sick student to work. The driver, together with three Taliban soldiers, return to the village and fetch Juma back to work.

Poor Juma really is very sick and can't do anything. I can tell he is not pretending, and I know that I must help my friend. I have come up with an idea I hope will be acceptable to the Taliban. "I will do double work today," I tell one of the Taliban men through my tears. "Please, can Juma go home? Please don't work him today," I continue.

"You care for this Juma greatly, I can see that," he says. "I will allow this, but never again." This lightens my heart, but burdens my little arms, as I have to move stone and wood for two of us. The work is difficult, but I have no choice. I have to do it, to help my friend—my first friend.

The day finally ends at sunset, and the Taliban tell us to go back to our homes. When I tell my family the events of the day, they cry—not tears of sadness, but of happiness. Baba says I am a greater man than any of the Taliban for helping Juma, and I know this is true.

For three months—the duration of my summer vacation from school—this work continues. We build the rooms. We know how hard this is, but we say nothing. And we don't usually talk much about the hard work when we are home. As students, we are afraid to say too much. The Taliban has made it clear that these rooms are not for any of us or our fellow villagers—these rooms are for the Taliban to live in. We are all so tired—exhausted, really—and sad from our three months of hard work to support the Taliban.

What makes everything worse is to return home at the end of the day only to find everyone in my family crying and saddened by the situation. But the three months have passed and now this work has ended. Tomorrow school starts, and I will learn the results of my exams. This good news helps me forget the labors of my summer vacation. I finish dinner and go to bed, full of excitement about what tomorrow might bring.

Next morning, I join up with Juma and finish my fifteen-minute walk to school with my friend.

"What do you think my results on the exam will be?" I ask him.

"You must be in first position, Hayat, for you are the brightest student." I trust him—Juma is always with me. Years later, Juma and I will sit together every day in Dubai.

When the teacher enters the class, he tells us that he will call one name at a time and give that student their results. I feel strongly that mine will be the first name called, since my position should be first, but it is not.

In fact, my name is never called.

Five students have not been called, from what I can tell, including me and Juma. What has happened? Naseeb Khan tells us all to wait for ten minutes, and he will return. Time passes slowly. Juma and I feel sad. We wonder if we did a bad job.

When our teacher returns, he brings with him three trophy cups and two notebooks.

I hear, "Hayatullah is in first position. Hayatullah, come for the trophy!"

I am very happy. I can't wait to show my trophy to my mom and Baba. Juma is in second position. And now I am even happier because Juma gets a trophy too.

Our first day back at school passes quickly. Juma and I walk the road home together, holding our trophies, and parting where the road diverges. When I arrive home, Mom is so happy she even cries a little. But I know that this is happy crying and not the crying she has been doing lately because of the Taliban. At lunch the rest of my family congratulates me, but I just listen while I eat.

My youngest sister asks me why she can't go to school. I tell her she is not allowed because of the Taliban. They do not allow girls to go to school. I think about how many things I have seen and learned at school, and I wish there was school for my sister. I stop eating for a minute to think about someday walking to school with my sister. I say nothing, but instead finish my lunch.

Chapter Two
October 2001

Time moves forward, never waiting for me. I'm now ten years old and in my second year of school. It seems everyone is talking about Osama bin Laden and America. We have no TV to see what is happening, so I don't have my own ideas about any of this. I just notice that people are getting really serious, and I sense things are happening differently around me as I walk to school. People have fear in their hearts. Everyone is afraid something terrible is going to happen.

We hear the Americans are attacking Afghanistan, so the people in my village have been busy preparing hiding places in the jungle and digging small caves in the mountains. Families throughout the village hide their gold and valuables by burying them underground in the mountains nearby. We will flee to these hiding places if we have to, and live in them for as long as it takes for us to be able to return safely to our village. In the Soviet-Afghan war from 1979 to 1989, people lived in their cave for six or seven months at a time. I know that my own family also has gold and other expensive stones, so I tell my Baba that we should hide this from the Americans, just as everyone else is doing.

"The Americans are not fighting us," says Baba, "they are fighting the Taliban. I have heard this on the radio. You must remember this." Baba then becomes very serious. "I am sorry to tell you, but I have only ten days left on my visa and I need to return to Dubai."

My head swims with thoughts of everything that is happening around me: Baba leaving, hiding gold in the mountains, an American attack. I just want my brain to shut off. I want to play in the trees with Juma and follow the birds. I resolve to find Juma, knowing he will take my mind off the matters of the world around me. As I move to leave, the Taliban suddenly blare out over the mosque loudspeaker.

The harsh voice "invites" everyone in the village to the Sarobi District the next day to attend a town meeting. The Taliban have arranged this meeting in Sarobi to inform people that America is attacking Afghanistan. I do not know what to think, but my Uncle Marjan and Baba believe the Taliban will give us information about the war between America and Afghanistan, and decide that we will leave the village tomorrow to attend this meeting. I don't understand what is happening in my village and in my big country, but I am curious nonetheless.

As occurs with most important topics, we discuss the upcoming meeting at dinner. Mom has cooked a delicious Kabuli rice, and it steams warmly from our bowls as Baba describes his urgency for returning to Dubai.

"But Baba," I ask brashly, "if you go to Dubai, then what will we do here, because we have no one in the home except my dumb Uncle Marjan?"

"Not being able to speak and not being able to hear do not make your Uncle Marjan dumb. Anyway, my brother Ibrahim will come from Dubai and he will stay with you while I am away."

Upon hearing this, I feel a little better. "Okay, but what do we do if the war comes to us?"

"The war will not come here. The Americans want to destroy the Taliban, not our village," he reassures me.

The next morning a banging on our door interrupts our breakfast. A bearded man, someone I don't recognize, tells us that we—and the rest of our village—must cook food for the Taliban's town meeting. Of course nobody in the village wants to cook for them, but we also know that we have no choice. At that, Mom starts preparing to cook before she has even finished her morning meal.

Before we depart for the meeting, Baba tells me, "Don't trust anything the Taliban say. They are not going to tell us the truth."

I laugh and ask, "Then why we are going?"

My father looks down and I know this is nothing to joke about. He replies, "If we don't go, they will take us to jail. So, we will go to the town meeting, listen to their lies for a half hour, and then return in time for the afternoon."

* * *

To be safe, we arrive at the meeting early. Although I do not say so aloud, I know I do not want to be there if my curiosity is going to be answered with dishonesty. The Taliban address the crowd gathered from a stage. They tell us that America wants to capture Afghanistan and that they will destroy the Taliban government if they do.

At this declaration, I feel overwhelming joy. Could the Americans actually rid us of the Taliban government? I look around and notice the smiling eyes of most everyone present, despite heads nodding in agreement with the Taliban speakers.

Baba leans down to tell me, "Trust only those words, that 'America will destroy the Taliban government.'" The Taliban continue talking about many things, but with their earlier pronouncement, I feel I have heard all that I need to hear. Then I hear the name *Osama bin Laden*. "Who is Osama?" I ask Baba.

"Just a moment, Hayat, and you will find out. The Taliban will introduce this man to us all." Baba was right. A Taliban spokesman then holds up a large picture of a man and tells us that this is Osama bin Laden. They explain that Osama is hiding in Afghanistan, and America wants to kill him. But they, the Taliban, will do everything possible to protect him.

Everyone is curious as to why the Americans want to kill Osama. The Taliban respond by telling us that he used airplanes to destroy two big buildings and this angered America. The Taliban on stage take no more questions. Instead, they invite us to go into the District, where they will feed us lunch. I know their lunch invitation is not something they are doing out of the kindness of their heart or because they care for us. We, along with our neighbors, have been forced to cook all this food. It is not the Taliban who are hosting us.

I look around and see all the people there—strangers, many who traveled from other villages like my own across my big country. I don't think they wanted to come here, but I know that if they are at all like us, they had no real say in this decision either. Like us, they must also listen to the Taliban.

I turn to my father and say, "Can we eat at home with Mom and my sisters, Baba? Mom cooked this food for the Taliban and I don't want to eat their food."

Baba looks at me and says, "Yes, we are going home for lunch because there are too many people here." He tells me to hold his hand tightly so he won't lose me in the crowd of strangers. Holding my father's hand is not a problem for me, because I don't want to lose him and end up with the Taliban. My thoughts go to the baby bird my mom made me return to its nest and family. I stay glued to my father's side the whole way home, not straying in the least.

Mom cooks another meal—this time, our family lunch. Familiar faces and Mom's fresh bread help erase the morning's somber shadow. I feel better being home, although the specter of the Taliban and Osama bin Laden are ever present.

* * *

Baba goes to the small market in the Sarobi District the next morning. He purchases everything we will need at home while he is away in Dubai. Usually he buys just food, such as vegetables and rice. But he is also concerned that an American attack is very close at hand, and he wants to prepare the household for that as well.

Everything is happening so quickly and the mood in our house is so serious that I just don't understand it all. Baba going to Dubai, Osama being hunted by the Americans, the Taliban making so many demands of us—these are big problems for such a little boy, and I struggle to sleep that evening. I think about going to the Sarobi District with Baba the next morning, as he will leave from there for Dubai. I know that if I go to school, I will miss my Baba. But if I go with Baba, then I will miss school.

Mom, in the way only a mother can, senses my struggle. I don't know what to do or feel as she looks at me lying in bed. Quietly she asks what is bothering me.

"I'm fine, Mom," I say.

She knows I'm upset about something and tells me to share my concern with her. I tell her I'm confused about what is happening around me. I don't know if I should try to go with Baba to the Sarobi District or stay home and go to school. She tells me that I should go with my father, which makes me happy. My mind is now at ease and I fall asleep quickly, as I know I need to wake up early the next morning.

* * *

Morning comes quickly—too quickly. Mom wakes me up and I head straight to the shower. After that, the family eats breakfast together.

Baba, who by now is aware of my difficult decision between going to school that day and going with him to the Sarobi District, tells me, "Hayat, keep your brain busy on studying. The world's troubles demand your studies."

My mind continues to race with questions about Osama and the war, and I say, "Okay, Baba. But what if America kills us during the war? What if we are all dead when you return? Where will you go because you will have no family?"

Upon hearing my questions, Baba's eyes tear up. I can tell he is about to cry, but he controls himself and assures me that America is not going to kill us. He reiterates that they are fighting the Taliban. I have much more to ask, but Mom gives me an angry look and says, "Finish your breakfast, Hayat, as you need to leave soon for the Sarobi District." Her stern tone silences further questions from me. I understand that Baba has his own troubles, so I remain silent as we finish breakfast.

After breakfast, Baba, my Uncle Marjan, and I pile into our Toyota truck and, after a few goodbyes, we head toward the Sarobi District. Marjan cannot talk or hear, but he is smart nonetheless, and can drive any car. On the way, I talk to Baba, just doing the blah-blah-blah of a nervous child, but he listens to every word. When we arrive in the Sarobi District, Baba walks to a transportation center while I wait with Uncle Marjan in the car. Five minutes later, Baba finds a taxi and talks with the driver, who tells him he needs only one more person to fill up the taxi and depart.

Baba returns to where my uncle and I are waiting and explains that he is going with the driver to Wanah, in the Pakistan province of Waziristan. From there he will continue to Deira Ismail Khan and then on to Karachi. After that, he will have to go to Dubai by airplane. These names do not mean much to me, for the world is big and full of unknown places, but I know that I will miss my Baba while he is away. Before getting into the taxi, Baba kisses me and hugs my Uncle Marjan. He then hands me one hundred rupees (approximately one U.S. dollar)—a veritable treasure for a young boy! We say our final goodbye to Baba as he climbs into the taxi. I don't bring it up with Baba, but I worry if my other uncle will arrive in time to protect us during the upcoming war with the Americans. Alas, Baba's brother did not arrive in time to travel back home with us.

Marjan starts the truck for our long, silent drive home. The only conversation taking place goes on inside my head, as I try to make sense of what is to come. Eventually I doze, and awaken only when Marjan parks the truck at home.

The warm sleepiness is chased out of my eyes quickly, as I see that Juma has been waiting for me. I'm so happy to see Juma, as I can share my concerns with him.

Juma asks, "Why did you not come to school today?"

"I was with my Baba," I reply. "He's going to Dubai for business today. He will be gone for some time." I grow sad upon hearing myself speak these words.

Juma listens, then asks, "Okay, but who is going to take care of your family?"

The uncle who was supposed to come from Dubai—Baba's other brother—to stay with us never made it, and so we have no man in our house to take care of our family. In spite of that, the words pour from my heart. "We have Allah and no one can take care of our family better than Allah." This satisfies us both, and nothing else is said about my Baba or Dubai as we eat lunch and then go out to play in our jungle till we both tire of playing and return home our usual separate ways.

That night, I explain to my Uncle Marjan all that I know about how America is coming to Afghanistan to attack Osama bin Laden. This is difficult, as he can't talk or hear, but he is very smart, and I think he understands me. Now that Baba has left, all we have in our home is this uncle of mine, and that must suffice. We enjoy our usual dinner routine and I decide to go to bed early as I have school in the morning. Sleep comes easily that night, for I am wiped out from such a long day.

* * *

Morning arrives and I listen for the usual sounds of my Baba moving about the house, but hear nothing. Then I remember he is gone. Why does he work so far away in this place called Dubai? I get myself ready for school and hurry out of the house, skipping and kicking stones as I make my way. In just a few short minutes, I will see my friend Juma and be back at school again that day. As I get closer to school I look for Juma, but instead I see that our teacher is standing outside the school ready to make an important announcement for us all to hear. Everyone gathers around the teacher, Juma and I standing side by side.

"Students," says my teacher, "this is to be your last day of school. The Americans will be arriving shortly—tomorrow, the day after—it makes no difference. They will be arriving, and we must suspend school during this time. We do not know what they will bring. We do not know what they will do. We have decided that you must all be with your families during this uncertain time. We look forward to reopening school and welcoming you all back as soon as it is safe to do so."

I can't believe what I am hearing—it's our last day of school? I can only think about the fact that Baba is far away and the Americans are arriving soon. We scatter in all directions, everyone running home upon hearing this news. I don't hear anything or anyone else. I hear only my teacher's words over and over, "The Americans are coming tomorrow. The Americans are coming tomorrow."

The date is October 5, 2001, and the entire village is getting ready to leave their home and hide in the mountains. Everyone is preparing to take shelter in the mountains, but my mom tells me we are not going anywhere.

Fear hits me hard when I hear her say this, and I argue back, "The Americans are coming and they will kill us!"

She responds by saying, "Do you trust your Baba?"

"Yes, I do," I say.

"Then we are not going anywhere. Your Baba already told you that the Americans are not coming to fight civilians. We will stay here. We will not fight, and we will not be killed by the Americans. They want the Taliban gone, just as much as we do."

My Baba has never given me a reason to not trust him, so these words calm me. However, by the end of the next day, after hearing the news about the Americans, most of the people in the village have fled to the mountains. It is night time and the village is completely dark. We do not turn on our own lights, as we do not want to bring attention to ourselves. Only darkness and silence surround us. It is quiet as we eat dinner in the dark. It is quiet as I lay in my bed. We remain silent throughout the morning, day, and night. I am afraid to speak in my own home, even though my home has no Taliban and I should feel free to speak. Everyone is full of worry.

Throughout all of this we are unable to communicate with Baba in Dubai. We have no phone, but this is normal in our village. When Baba is away and we want to communicate with him—for any reason at all—we record a cassette tape for him. We then wait until we hear that someone is going to Dubai, and we give them the cassette to take it to my Baba. This is everyone's normal way of communicating to those who are far away, and we do this without thinking twice or thinking our lives are made more difficult because of it. We do this because we are unaware of the many differences between us and the rest of the big world.

We expect the Americans will arrive the next day and the fighting will begin. So far, we have been lucky because our province has not been bombed, but this does not lighten our hearts this night. Thoughts of dying and bombing are constant. When we awake in the morning everything seems normal in our house, but the inaction of the village is foreign. There are no sounds and no people, no movement and no traffic. Just as yesterday, we eat breakfast in silence, our fear a constant cloud hanging over our heads. Mom's eyes are red and she complains she has a bad headache. I sense she could break down in tears at any moment, but I can tell she is hiding her tears from us all—from me, my sisters, and my Uncle Marjan.

Mom does not want us to be scared, but she was here during the Russian war and knows what can happen when the Americans attack. The Russians did not object to killing civilians or anyone else during that war. I sometimes wonder why the Russians had to kill us. Did they have friends here who died, and their killings were in retaliation? Did the Russians simply think all Afghanis should die? What did we do to deserve that? All I want in life is to wake up in the morning, eat Mom's breakfast, go to school, and play with Juma. I think about the baby birds and wonder how many of our birds from the jungle were killed by Russians.

After breakfast, I tell Mom I am going out to the village. At those words, she can no longer hold back her tears and says, "Don't go anywhere, Hayat. We have to stay together. If the time comes, we must all die together."

Her tone scares me worse than any foreign soldiers could and, through my own tears, I say, "I don't want to die. I didn't do anything wrong!" Now everyone in our little house is crying.

Just then I remember something important. "Mom, the radio! Let's turn on the radio," I say. Maybe we will hear where the fighting started and that the Americans are not coming to kill us.

Mom agrees the time is right to use the radio and turns it on. She spins the dial slowly, trying to find a Pashto radio station. Eventually, she finds one. Finally! News from the outside, and we listen intently for reports on the fighting. We hear that bombing has begun on the city of Kabul, but we still don't know if they are bombing civilians or the Taliban.

Suddenly, over the sounds of the radio, we hear people moving about outside our house. I feel myself go pale with fear, as I can only think that the American soldiers are here and they are going to kill us. Mom goes to the door to look outside, and sees the disturbance is not from soldiers, but from the villagers returning from the mountains! A line of my neighbors and friends is winding down the mountain trails, and this dispels all my fears. I am happy when I realize we are not going to die after all. Mom now looks happy too. We are no longer alone in the village. She urges me to go out to learn the truth about the Americans, to find out if they are fighting us or the Taliban.

After several days of being stuck inside the house, I am more than happy to run free in my village. I quickly find that everyone is talking about the war, but I am also confused because everyone is saying something different. Finding any sort of consistent truth is impossible. Some people say the Americans are destroying innocent peoples' homes; others claim they are only targeting Taliban buildings. Nobody has any definitive answers or proof of any of this, so I return home with nothing but rumors and wild claims.

When I arrive back home, Mom is busy cooking lunch. I go the kitchen and tell her the different stories everyone was telling and that I was unable to find the truth in any of what I heard.

"Son, there are no truths in war," she tells me, and hands me a bowl of rice and vegetables. The greatest truth for me, right now, is that I am hungry after a long morning of gathering non-information. Another truth? Mom's lunch tastes better when the village is full of people.

After lunch, we all take a rest, as we had not slept well the night before. This rest will be a bit more peaceful knowing our neighbors have returned home, but we remain fearful from our lack of knowledge about the war and wondering still if the Americans will kill us all.

* * *

When darkness falls, we look out and see a few dots of orange from meager fires located high up on the mountainside. Some people from our village have remained in the caves. I feel a little better that night with other people in the village, but decline to eat dinner, as I am not hungry. Even though things appear somewhat normal, I have no appetite.

I am tired and go to bed, but my mind is racing with thoughts of everything that is happening. My Baba is still very far away, the Americans are still bombing my country, and the Taliban remain ever-present. I think about the events of the day, the silence of the village the past few days, and my family, alone, without Baba. My sleep is filled with terrifying nightmares. I see American jets bombing our village, destroying everything—civilians, Taliban—they do not know the difference. I see houses burning, with fire and flames everywhere. I notice a soldier advancing towards me. He has a large rifle and somehow I know that he is going to shoot me in the head, and the very moment he pulls the trigger, I wake up, shouting and crying out loud enough to wake up my whole family. Mom rushes to my side, offering comforting words, telling me that it was just a bad dream. I tell her I'm fine and ask for a glass of water. After satisfying my thirst, I manage to fall back to sleep and avoid that terrifying dreamscape of destruction.

When I awake in the morning, my world appears normal again. There are no sounds of bombing or fighting, but my nightmare from last night remains with me, and my brain still buzzes with faded mayhem. I feel that I must see with my own eyes that my dream wasn't reality—that the village is still standing, not smoldering. Like a timid mouse, I open the door to the outside world, and see it remains intact, untouched by the destruction that ran rampant through my night. I looked all around and found no visible proof of those awful things from my nightmare.

Relieved, I turn back inside and see Mom looking at me from the kitchen. She seems concerned, but I tell her everything is fine outside. With this said, I realize I am hungry and ask my mother for breakfast. As I eat, I recall my dream to my mother. Surprisingly, she smiles and tells me that this dream means the Americans will never bomb our village, and that we will be safe until the end.

I am reluctant to believe her, and say, "I hope so, but I don't think so. They shot me in my dream. They bombed the entire village. Am I completely wrong?" I thought that what I had dreamt had occurred in real life. The nightmare made me lose control of myself and my emotions, and was, in fact, one of the worst dreams I had ever had.

"That was only a dream, Hayat, and there are worlds of difference between dreams and our world. Your dream was based in fear, not that which will happen. Your father told us we would be safe. So far, we have been, and that must strengthen you," she tells me. "Now, go find Juma. Surely his family has returned." My mother's words have given me comfort, and I head out in search of my friend.

My little village has returned to life. As I walk the familiar path to Juma's house I see many people have moved back from the mountains into their houses. The smells of breakfasts cooking, cries of young children, and even the roar of a motorcycle are welcome attacks on the emptiness that held us captive just two days earlier.

When I reach Juma's house, I discover that it is still abandoned and closed up. His house is in the jungle where it is surrounded by big trees and birds of all sorts. I realize that Juma and his family must be hiding out somewhere in the jungle or in the cave they built. I decide to wait, thinking that perhaps they might see me. Suddenly, out of the total silence, I hear Juma call my name.

I know they remain hidden because they think our village has been overtaken by American soldiers, so I call out, "Juma, I can't see you, but it is just me! Please come out! Nobody is here except me!"

I have convinced them to trust me, and soon enough I see Juma coming toward me from between a few large trees, pale faced and crying. His fear is apparent, and it frightens me. "Why are you so scared?" I ask.

"Did they kill your family?" Juma asks. "I don't want to die."

I do my best to calm his fears. "Everyone is fine. I have just come from my house and the village is safe. You can return home."

Upon hearing this, Juma's face regains its normal color and he hugs me. "Then, come with me, to my family," he says. "Tell them we can go back home."

At first I tell him to go get his family, but Juma insists I go to the cave with him. Together we go to where Juma's family is still hiding, suspicious of every sound and movement.

Just as it was with Juma, his family doesn't fully believe me when I tell them it is safe to return home. I tell them that my family heard on the radio that the Americans will not bomb civilians. Although I don't know for certain if this is true, I am able to convince them, with Juma insisting I would never deceive him. I help them carry their belongings back to their home, where they are so happy to see the village is filling back up. For my help, Juma's mother allows him to come to my house so that we may spend the afternoon together.

On the way to my house, I tell Juma all about my dream and all the bad things that came to me in the night.

"This is a really bad dream," he tells me, in contradiction to what my mom said earlier.

"I know this is a bad dream, but my mom doesn't think so. What do you think it means?" I ask.

Just as I am uncertain about the meaning of my dream, so is Juma. He tells me he does not know.

As we reach my house, I see my mother waiting for me at the door. She is angry that I was gone so long, but she does not scold me because Juma is with me. She is surprised to learn that Juma's family returned home just this morning.

"Mom, would we be able to have some Kabuli rice?" I ask, even though it is not yet lunchtime.

Mom agrees and gets to work cooking our lunch. Suddenly, we hear a thunderous roar, and recognize it as the sound of airplanes. We look up to see a clear sky, but then something streaks high across the sky. We have never seen a fighter jet, but we immediately recognize it as such. Thankfully the jet did nothing to our village, but just crossed over on its way to bomb the Burmool District. Burmool is the last district of Paktika Province on the Pakistan border, and is very close to Waziristan in Pakistan. There is always trouble there, but at this young age I don't understand why.

The loud, frightful sound of the jet shook my entire body. And, even though the jet did not attack our village, panic takes over everywhere. Houses suddenly empty as everyone runs to the mountains to take cover in the caves they have dug for themselves. This time, Mom makes us go too. Together with my sisters and Juma, we all run out of our house. I don't know where Uncle Marjan is. He would not have heard the fighter jets, so it's possible he was left behind. We are halfway to our cave when Mom remembers our uncle and tells us she must run back to get him. And soon we all make it safely to a tiny cave where we remain for a time.

* * *

Nighttime in a mountainside cave is harsh. I am cold and cry out of fear and hunger, for we had raced out of our house without lunch. It is then that I am reminded of how smart my mother is. In our haste, she was able to grab provisions to make us some food, and we soon find ourselves huddled around a small fire where she is cooking our Kabuli rice.

After dinner my mother looks for a way to block off the entrance to the cave, to keep us safe from wild animals. Before the Soviet-Afghan war, lions and tigers roamed the mountains. Now, although fewer of those most dangerous animals remain in our mountains, other predators such as wolves and wild dogs are continually on the hunt. Mom uses her shawl to cover the cave entrance as best she can. Once this small bit of protection is in place, we try to fall asleep. Juma and I are exhausted from the day's events, as are my sisters, but there is not enough room for us to all lie down, so we must try to sleep sitting up. Despite the cold and discomfort, I am able to eventually fall asleep.

Before I know it, it is morning and Mom tells us we are going back home.

"No! The Americans will kill us," I shout, scared for my life.

"We will all die anyway if the Americans start bombing, so we will leave the cave and go back home," she says.

I think about my mother's words. Even though she is forcing us to leave the safety of the cave, I know I don't want to die here like some kind of frightened animal. "You are right, Mom," I tell her. "If we are to die, it is better they kill us in our own home."

Without Baba, the combined strength of my mother's voice and my own suffices to stir my sisters. And Juma, of course, follows me without question.

After the long trek down the mountain we arrive back home. The village remains mostly empty of residents, but I feel it will soon fill up since we haven't heard any jets all morning. Juma, my mom, my sisters, and I sit together, praying to Allah to save our small village.

We soon realize Allah heard our prayers because something great has happened. The government's district employees were Taliban from Pakistan, but now they are all gone and their district offices are closed. There are no Taliban anywhere in the district! Allah really listened and responded to our prayers.

As darkness approaches, Juma says he wants to go home, but we convince him to stay with us for one more night. His family is surely safe and I tell him I will walk back to his home with him in the morning. He agrees, and we fall asleep, feeling warmer than the previous night in the cave.

The next morning, Juma and I head back to Juma's house. "My parents are probably very worried about where I've been all this time," he says.

I agree, thinking about how worried my Baba and mother would be if I were gone for two days without word.

When we reach Juma's house, we realize his parents were more than just worried—they are furious at us.

"It has been two days since you showed up and lured us out of our cave," Juma's dad yells. "It has been two days since we saw our son!"

"Juma stayed with us while we hid in the mountains. He was safe with us in our cave. The jets are not coming for us, they are going to Burmool District. It is safe now in the village."

I leave Juma. I know he will make things better between us.

* * *

Normal life continues for the next two weeks. We do not see any more jets or American soldiers, but we know the war continues in Afghanistan's big cities. One day, I am out playing with my friends. We see helicopters approach our village and stop to watch as they fly over. They fly low at first and then rise back up in the sky, as if they are playing with us. They do not shoot at the children who race after them. They do not bomb our houses. We realize the reports we have heard all along must be true—the Americans are not attacking civilians! The helicopter leaves us and returns to the American camp that I heard is in the Burmool District of Paktika Province.

Back at home, I tell my mother about our adventures with the helicopters, and that they did not shoot at us. She was so happy to hear this news. This makes me want to forget the day we ran for our mountain cave where we slept on the cold hardness of the cave floor.

"Hayat, of course, if the Americans did not shoot people from the helicopter then they are not going to kill civilians," she tells me. "I remember the Russians were shooting civilians from helicopter gunships."

* * *

A few days later we hear that American soldiers are renting homes in Abaskheel, a village to the east of us where they will build their camp. Everyone is talking about this as the stories fly through the whole village. A man named Hazarat rented his home, and shifted his family to another village. He was paid one hundred thousand dollars from the Americans for this!

Juma and I are eager to see the Americans in the home of Hazarat. Our curiosity, which is really more nosiness than anything, gets satisfied, and we are amazed at the sum of money Hazarat was paid for the use of his home. But what we really want to see is an American face. We are fascinated and want to find out as much as we can about the Americans. The Taliban told us that the face of an American is different from our face. They told us Americans have red faces. And so, Juma and I decide to take the long walk to where the Americans are staying in order to see the soldiers.

As we approach Hazarat's house, I am surprised when I see the Americans. The soldiers stand outside the house, carrying weapons, but they smile and act friendly as we get closer. They don't look anything like what the Taliban described. The only difference is they are dressed in military uniforms, and we are wearing our long tunic tops over trousers. They don't have red faces! Upon seeing all this, Juma and I are no longer afraid or apprehensive.

We laugh, and they laugh back as we try to communicate with each other. We don't understand English and they don't understand Pashto. Even their translators can't fully understand Pashto because they speak only Farsi. Later, when I recall this first encounter with the American forces, I still don't see how anyone thought Farsi would help in the Paktika Province of Afghanistan. "Someone needs a geography lesson," I always say.

Amazingly enough, between our joking around and poor translations, Juma and I figure out that the translator is telling us the American soldiers would like to visit our village. This excites us greatly.

"Sure. Yes!" we answer without hesitation. The soldiers tell us it is time for us to return home and that they will visit the next day. We hurry home, anxious to prepare our village for the soldiers' arrival. Along the way, Juma and I chatter about how loud their trucks will be, how our neighbors will react to these foreign men, and how everyone will be so surprised to see how the Americans really look.

Juma and I finally feel safe and happy once again. Back at the village, we tell our story to everyone we see. They can hardly believe what they're hearing. Eventually Juma and I end up on his side of the village to eat dinner with his family. Juma's family joins our excitement about the

Americans coming to our village the next day, and we have a very lively meal.

* * *

Juma arrives early the next morning, before Mom can finish serving us breakfast. All morning long, we wait for the American soldiers, but they do not come. We run through the village and see how many people are out and about, waiting to see if the Americans will actually show up. By two o'clock, however, the crowds disperse, as it is clear the Americans will not be visiting our village after all.

As the day grows late, everybody heads to our mosque for prayer. There is still no sign of the Americans, and we hear some sneers and laughs aimed at us. Did we imagine this interaction? Did the soldiers lie to us? Maybe we just misunderstood the translator, and the American soldiers are not coming at all. After prayer I go home, confused about what is happening, but these thoughts dissipate when I get home and see Sobia waiting for me at the door. She tells me that my Uncle Ibrahim has arrived from Dubai. I'm happy to have him with us at our house, given that my Baba isn't here. I go inside to greet Uncle Ibrahim, and the very first thing I ask him is, "What did you bring me from Dubai?"

"A bicycle," he says. I can't believe my ears, because I have never had a bicycle. I can't wait to see it and try it for the first time, but my uncle tells me we must first take the bicycle to a shop in the Sarobi market. "They must assemble it and prepare it for you, little Hayat."

"But the Sarobi market is closed," I cry out. "What about Uncle Marjan? He may be mute, but he is smart and can surely fix my bike!"

My Uncle Ibrahim and I remove all the pieces from the various bags for my Uncle Marjan. The day has changed into night, but I press for my uncle to finish building my bicycle. And so he does.

I look at my bicycle, so shiny and new, and am so excited to get on it and ride, even though it is dark outside. I realize, however, there is a problem beyond the lack of light—I don't know how to ride! Uncle Marjan tries to help me for a short time, before we must go in for dinner. He holds the cycle for me as I get onto the seat, then he pushes me along the way. These first attempts at riding are difficult for me, and Uncle

Marjan quickly tires. Uncle Ibrahim tells me to park the bicycle for the day and go inside for dinner.

"Juma will help me learn to ride," I say.

Early the next morning, I run the whole way to Juma's home, excited to tell him the news of my Uncle Ibrahim's present. "Juma, my uncle brought me a bicycle from Dubai," I spit out between heavy breaths, "But, I don't know how to ride, so you will help me learn?"

"Really? A new bicycle," he asks, almost in awe of what I am telling him. "I can't wait to see it, Hayat. Let me ask my mother if I can stay all day. Maybe I can even spend the night with your family?"

"Of course! This will be a great day," I tell him.

After getting permission from his parents, Juma and I run back to my house. His eyes open wide when he first sees it. He loves my new bicycle, and I tell him it is for both of us. "You can ride it any time you want, Juma," I tell my best friend. We both laugh at this however, because neither of us knows how to ride a bicycle!

We spend the entire day trying to master the bicycle, supporting each other as we find our balance and helping each other up after we fall. Learning to ride a bike is a difficult thing, much harder than we think. Dusty and bruised, we go home when night arrives. Without lights in our village, it is completely dark, and we give up trying to ride for the day. My sisters and uncle tease us at dinner that night, but we remain determined to learn how to ride. After dinner, we say goodnight and go to bed, vowing that we will be able to ride without any problem by the end of the next day.

* * *

The next morning, Juma and I walk the bicycle into the village, ready to pick up where we left off the night before. As excited as we are at the prospect of practicing our bicycle riding, imagine our excitement upon seeing a pair of large mud-colored trucks entering our village at the same time. I have never seen cars like this before, and am a bit frightened by them. Is this the Taliban with some new weapons, or the Americans who never showed up two days earlier? One of the doors opens, and we immediately recognize the men who step out as American soldiers. Juma and I practically read each other's mind. We are both anxious to talk to the Americans again, and so we return the bike to my house, let my family know the Americans have arrived, and race back to see the soldiers.

By now many villagers have stepped out of their homes to see what is going on. The Americans have stopped their cars near our village mosque, which was built after the Russian war, and they remove boxes from their cars. Quickly enough, we realize they have brought supplies for us. From morning till night the Americans hand out supplies to the people of the village—food, water, toys for children, books in English, pens, and notebooks. They provide new, blue school bags for students. A few people wonder if the food the Americans give to us is halal. That is, is it permissible to eat according to our Islamic laws? They go to the imam of the mosque to see if the food is halal. The imam looks at the pictures of the food and the labels in Arabic on the back of the packages. He pronounces that every product says that the food is halal, which pleases us greatly.

I help my Uncles Marjan and Ibrahim carry the goods back to our home. My mom and sisters are overjoyed at the amount of food we have brought with us. I show my mother that I also have everything I need for school, but school is still closed.

At dinner that night I talk to my Uncle Ibrahim. We are all so happy and thankful for what the Americans have given us, and I have my new bicycle from Dubai and my new school bag, notebooks and English books, but something is missing, I tell my uncle. I have been without school for too long. My uncle agrees, and says he will discuss this with the rest of the village while he is at the mosque the next day. At that good news, I sleep peacefully that night.

I accompany Uncle Ibrahim into the village the next morning. He wants to meet my teacher to talk about the school, so I find Naseeb Khan and introduce them. After some discussion, my teacher agrees that it is safe enough to reopen the school. He asks my uncle to tell everyone at the mosque that school will be reopening, or to tell the imam, who will then tell everyone in the village that school is opening again.

My uncle and I celebrate the good news by going into one of the village shops where he allows me to choose a cake. I select the same cake

I bought so long ago, when I first met Juma. I feel as if I am safe with my Uncle Ibrahim, and I'm very happy because our school will start again in the morning. I can't wait to go back to school. It seems such a long time since I was last at school, and I feel like I must continue to learn about the big world around me.

In the afternoon, I take my bicycle out to ride again but I continue to fall down without making any progress in learning how to ride. I try and try and, after a bloodied elbow, scraped-up palms, and torn pair of pants, succeed at riding a few yards at a time. Before I know it, the day has flown by, and evening prayers are called for. Uncle Ibrahim leaves for the mosque. I wait anxiously for the imam's announcement that school will re-start, and am rewarded when he goes over the loudspeakers to tell the village we will begin school again the next day. We, and everyone else, are overjoyed to hear this news.

"I wish my uncle would hurry up and return home," I say.

"Why?" asks my mother.

"So that we can eat dinner and I can get ready for school tomorrow."

* * *

We have one hundred and fifty boys in eight classes, each class a different grade level, and only two teachers to teach us all. After finishing all eight levels, students go to school in the Urgun District for four years and then to the university. At school I hear the name Hamid Karzai repeatedly. Many people agree that this man will become president of Afghanistan now that the Taliban are no longer in control.

A lot of my friends and neighbors go to Kabul to see Karzai when this becomes official. My Uncle Ibrahim and I leave for Kabul on December 15. We reach Ghazni Province at midnight and stay until morning. The highway that takes us directly into Kabul is full of holes and broken slabs, remnants from the fighting against the Russians and the Taliban. We finally reach Kabul and search for a hotel, but many of them were destroyed during the wars. And those that weren't destroyed, are already full. It seems as if my whole country is coming to Kabul to see Hamad Karzai, soon to be our new president, and we are left without a room as a result.

Uncle Ibrahim tells me not to worry, we will find a hotel. He asks for help from a taxi driver, who says he will help for a hundred rupees. We agree, and the taxi driver takes us to the Ariana Hotel, where we are able to book a room. The luxury and beauty of the hotel completely overwhelm me and I am awestruck as I look around. My modest home does not compare to this place. For dinner we order kabob, and afterwards go right to sleep.

My uncle and I spend the next two days in the city of Kabul. We don't do much except walk around and look at everything. I am amazed at what I see. And, when night falls at the end of our day, I am equally struck by the night life in Kabul. So many lights, so much noise and movement—nothing like the dark nights in my small village.

The day of Karzai's inauguration, December 22, the streets of Kabul are crowded with people and traffic. Uncle Ibrahim and I are at the jirga—the great assembly that installed Hamid Karzai as President of Afghanistan. We cannot see Karzai from where we stand, but we know it is over when the people around us start hugging and congratulating each other. We have a new president—not one who was elected, but one who stepped up and took over after the Taliban leader, Mullah Muhammad Omar, fled. Pictures of Hamid Karzai are distributed throughout the crowd so that, even if we can't see him, we know what he looks like. I have never seen so much joy, happiness, and hope in my people as I did the day Hamid Karzai became our president.

Uncle Ibrahim and I leave Kabul the next day. We drive for two days straight. Once back home, we tell our family and the others who remained in the village all about Kabul. They are a little disappointed that we did not meet our new president, but we show them the pictures of him. We leave a picture of him in the car so that we can show it to anyone wherever we go. Everyone who sees the picture says the president seems to be a good man.

President Karzai's message is for all Afghanis in every province across the country to stand with the government in Kabul and to work with the government. Baba and six cousins heed this call of duty, and they soon become police officers in the Sarobi District.

Chapter Three
Fall 2002

Before the start of winter, Uncle Ibrahim must leave us to return to Dubai. Soon my Baba will return home to us. As we did just a short while earlier, Marjan and I make the trip to the Sarobi District. But this time we ride with Uncle Ibrahim instead of Baba. My uncle will take a rental taxi from there to Burmool, then from Burmool to Wannah, Pakistan. Like my father, Uncle Ibrahim has a Pakistani passport which will allow him passage into that country. We will miss him, but the excitement of Baba coming home soon quashes a little bit of how I feel about Uncle Ibrahim leaving.

With my uncle gone, I keep myself busy with school and try not to think about Baba and when he will return. We, like the rest of the people in the village, have no phone, no easy way to communicate with Baba. This helps me focus on school and on becoming a good bicycle rider. Juma has been helping me with both. Not only do we practice riding the bike every day, but because Juma and I want the top two positions in school again this year, we prepare for our exams together. We spend our afternoons asking each other questions from every school book we have, with each trying to give the correct answers.

Before I know it, the end of the school year is here, and with it, our final exam day. Juma and I sit together and work on our respective exam papers. I finish first and hand mine in to my teacher. Juma is the next to turn in his paper. The teacher immediately begins correcting and marking our papers. Juma and I sit quietly while the other students complete their exams. When the last student has turned in his exam, our teacher announces we have three months of vacation.

He laughs when he tells us, "Do not work for the Taliban this vacation." Although the teacher was trying to joke, his words bring back the horrible memories of last summer, of how Juma, the other students, and I were forced to build houses for the Taliban. I've been able to forget it for the most part, but my teacher's words sting as much as the hard slap I was given the day Juma was out sick.

Of course, everyone is glad the Taliban no longer control our district. And, this vacation, instead of hauling bricks and rocks, Juma and I are able to go to the American soldiers' camp every day. Since Juma and I have mastered the bicycle, we get to the camp faster than anyone else, and we do this all summer. Walking to the camp took about thirty minutes, and we get there in even less time on the bicycle. We manage to learn some English words, along with the entire alphabet, all the way to the letter Z. Juma and I are grateful to these soldiers, and thank them every day. We see that, despite how busy the Americans are, they take time to teach us and occasionally play with us. Some of them even show us pictures of America, of their families and children!

One night, a couple of weeks into the summer, my family and I hear the sounds of a car nearing our home. Because I no longer worry about the Taliban in our area, I go to the door and throw it open to see who it is. Imagine how happy I am when I see my Baba! I run to him and throw myself into his arms. He gives me a big hug back and is amazed at how much I have grown. He tells me to help him with the bags he has brought back from Dubai. I gladly oblige, hoping that one of them has something for me. Once we carry his things into our house, I ask Baba what he would like for dinner, but he asks only for water. Mom tells him that is not enough, and that she will cook for him, but he says he is tired and just wants to sleep. He must be exhausted, I think. In the end, we all go straight to bed. I look forward to the next day, when we will all be able to talk to Baba.

I wake up happy the next morning, and go to see if Baba is awake yet. He is, and we head out for breakfast. While eating, Baba asks me if Hamid Karzai's government is better than the Taliban's. I tell him that the Karzai government is a hundred times better than the Taliban. "I just hate the Taliban," I tell him, making my position very clear. I know exactly how much my father dislikes the Taliban, and my answers please him. We continue talking about Dubai, school, Juma, and the bicycle. Then Baba tells me that he is planning to build us a new home. This is big news, and I should probably be excited to hear it, but I respond with a simple "okay." Despite the grandness of this news, what I am really thinking about is riding my bicycle over to Juma's to play. Now that Baba is home, I feel completely happy and safe and, more than anything at that moment, ready to get Juma and go back to the American's camp. You see, Juma and I spend our mornings at the camp and return home at lunch time, and play together for the remainder of the afternoon.

Even with our routine, our summer vacation goes by quickly. Results Day finally arrives—the day we learn the results of our exams. Last year Juma came in second place behind me, and I pray we will repeat that success. That morning, we sit in the classroom, waiting nervously for the teacher to call us up to the stage. Doubts about my placement creep into my head until the teacher finally calls me up. On stage, he tells everyone that I, Hayat, am in first position for the second year in a row! Juma doesn't have to wait long to find out that he retains his second-place position. We are both very happy, of course, but I think our placements are odd, because the answers Juma and I gave on our exams were the same. I can only conclude that since I finished my exam first, I earned the first position.

When we return home I show my results to my family, and everyone congratulates me. They've seen how hard I study and feel I have truly earned this. Even though Baba wasn't here to see me work, he is just as proud and gives me five hundred rupees as a reward. I can't believe he gives me so much money, but I gladly accept it!

Chapter Four
2003

I can hardly believe I am already in my third year of school. Even as a young boy, I understand that time does not wait, and this year is turning out to be an eventful one. In January, the Americans start work building their first base in the Urgun District of the Paktika Province. By the end of April, the base is complete, and the Americans allow the people of Urgun to work on their base. In fact, most people in Urgun have changed jobs and now work at the base—even some who have never had jobs are allowed to work here, which is good for them.

October arrives, and with it, my baby brother enters the world. I cannot describe how happy this has made me. I am even able to convince my parents to allow me to name him. After a few days of thinking, I choose the name Sadiqullah. Everyone agrees. We decide to have a party to celebrate the birth of Sadiqullah. Since there is no Taliban in our village, we have the freedom to invite everyone we know.

In the past, the Taliban was a problem. Back when they governed our village, if someone got married or had a baby, the Taliban prohibited any type of party, dancing, or music to celebrate these happy events. The most they allowed us was the sacrifice of a large animal for a feast meal. That may seem relatively generous on their part, but the Taliban was actually more interested in partaking in the feast on our account. Understand, the Taliban were never a part of our village family, but expected to be treated as such. People who could afford the animal for slaughter were also expected to give the Taliban money. The Taliban were supposedly the government, but they took from the village people instead of providing anything for us. It is not that the Taliban needed our slaughtered animals or money; they just liked to take from us whenever they could.

Our party to celebrate the arrival of Sadiqullah will be simple. We will sacrifice a goat, then cook it in our home. To this very day, I never have learned how to slaughter a goat, or any other animal for that matter. Years after Sadiqullah's birth, I once tried to slaughter a chicken. The bird ended up running all around the yard with me chasing after it. I haven't tried again since that debacle. My friend, who happened to be observing my chicken disaster, could not believe I did not know how to properly sacrifice an animal. He didn't bother to help, but just stood there and laughed at me. I told him I didn't know the reason, but no man in my family knows how to slaughter an animal, and so for Sadiqullah's party we enlist the help of one of our neighbors.

We invite all the families of the village to the party. There are six hundred homes in our village, many with multiple generations of family living together under one roof. My baba's mother lives in our house, and her husband, my grandfather, was killed by the Taliban. Since the Taliban is gone, our party will have dancing, but men may only dance in front of other men and women can only dance in the presence of women, so my family is now busy preparing two separate halls.

While Baba and Uncle Marjan go to the market to buy the goats that will be sacrificed, I ride my bicycle to Juma's to personally invite him and his family to the party. They are more than happy to join us, so Juma and I ride ahead of them and arrive just in time to see Baba returning from the market. He has brought not one, not two, but four goats home with him! I don't really want to see these beautiful goats sacrificed, but since we have invited so many people, we have to provide them all with a meal. Since no one in my family knows how to slaughter and prep the goats for cooking, Baba sends me to fetch one of the neighbors who can help with this task. By the time we return, I am now getting really excited for the party, and run and jump all through the house. But when it comes time for the goat slaughter to occur, Juma and I decide to go out to the farm, because we do not want to see the animals being slaughtered. We spend the afternoon playing, and keep away from all the work that is going on at home.

Guests begin to arrive at our home at sunset. We invite them in and serve them fresh, hot food, which everyone enjoys. They comment that my Baba must have picked out the best goats at the market. Of course our neighbors all want to see baby Sadiqullah, so once dinner is over, everyone cleans up and washes their hands. Mom then brings my brother out for everyone to admire.

Now it is time for singing and dancing. We play our taped music in the hall, just loud enough for people to hear it for dancing while still being able to talk to each other. The party continues until midnight, and I enjoy it tremendously—the dancing, the laughter, the way everyone is so friendly. This is the first real party of my life, and I like it.

At the end of the night, as Juma's parents get ready to leave, I ask them if Juma can spend the night at my house. They agree, even though we have school the next morning. We help clean up, then fall into bed, exhausted from the night's dancing and partying.

Somehow Juma and I sleep until ten o'clock the next morning. Baba says we don't have to go to school since it is so late, and this makes us both very happy. My oldest sister Sobia is now of age to help my mom, and she prepares breakfast for us, which we eat hungrily, and then make plans to go into the village so Juma can return home.

As soon as we step outside, we see helicopters coming around the mountains in the distance. A minute later, we watch as they start bombing in the mountains. We have no idea what is happening. This is the first time since the events of September 11, 2001, that the Americans have targeted the Taliban in our mountains. Our party of the night before seems like a dream, like it happened so long ago. Our friends and family, the very people we danced and ate with just hours earlier, are now running scared. Juma and I quickly go back to my house, where Baba tells us nobody can go outside. We hear the war go on and on and on, without any breaks in the bombing. In our own misery and fear we know we can do nothing to either stop this latest horror or protect ourselves.

Finally, midway through the afternoon, the helicopters fly back in the direction of the base at Urgun. Juma, worried about what his parents must be thinking, says he wants to go home. Even though I tell him he would be better off staying at our house, he insists on returning to his own family. I understand his desire, and so agree to ride him home on my bicycle. Together we head out and manage to get Juma safely back home without any problem. I had promised my parents that I would return back home right away, and so I did.

At dinner that night, we are all very quiet, wondering when the next episode of war and bombing will occur. I ask Baba why the Americans bombed the mountains. He explains that he has heard the Taliban have been hiding in the mountains and the Americans are still trying to kill them. This explanation makes me feel a bit better. I am happy that the Taliban are not trying to find shelter in our village, because I don't think we could tolerate all that violence again. I am also happy that my friends the Americans are working hard to eliminate the Taliban and make our land safe.

On my way to school the next day, I see American soldiers coming toward our village. I stop along my usual route to wait and see them, along with many others from my village. As they approach, they toss toys and chocolates to the children who line the street. Everyone is scrambling around, happy and excited, to collect as many of the treats as they can. I join the others and stuff my school bag with the treats the Americans throw out to us. I am so absorbed in this fun that I forget about school. But I am not the only one, as other students from my school have the same idea, and tag along behind the soldiers, hoping to get more goodies.

The soldiers pass through our village, most of them heading toward the mountains they bombed the day before. Two of them stay behind in the village, handing out more treats. With all this excitement, everybody misses school that day.

Back at home, I count up four toys and a mountain of chocolates, which I show off to my sisters. Two of the toys I give to my younger sisters and I keep the others for my little brother Sadiqullah, so that he may enjoy them when he is older. I save the chocolates for later too. I tell my older sister that I am hungry and ready to eat lunch, which she promptly prepares. After lunch I go back into the village to see the American soldiers who are still there with their bikes. The American's bikes are different from mine. Theirs have four tires, just like cars. Right away I see how much easier it must be to ride around on our rocky terrain on four tires instead of two.

The village is full of curious people, but no one says anything to the Americans, since no one speaks English. The adults just watch the soldiers, and occasionally a child approaches one in hopes of getting another toy or piece of candy. By four o'clock that afternoon, the remaining American soldiers return from the mountains. They stop cars in the village and tell the drivers there are still Taliban hiding in the mountains, and that no one should go into the mountains until they (the

Americans) have cleared all Taliban out. They will inform us when the area is clear of the Taliban. After a few hours of these warnings, the Americans go back to their camp, and the village onlookers disperse back to their own homes. I go to bed happy that night because I feel safer knowing the Americans are really fighting to push out the Taliban and also because I will definitely go to school the next day.

My happiness from the night before is quickly dispelled in school the next day. The teacher is mad at all the students for having missed school the day before. He is especially mad at me and Juma, because we are the top two students. We missed two days in a row! He tells us we must be leaders and demonstrate to all the other students just how important education is. We know he is right, and so we immediately focus on the day's lesson, studying and listening intently all morning long to our class on the Dari language. The hours fly by, and before I know it, it is 11:30. Our lessons end for the day, and we head back home.

As we walk our usual route, Juma and I discuss the possibility of having a girls' school in the village. We decide we must speak to our parents about our idea, and ask them to talk to the imam at our mosque about opening a girls' school. I am sure my Baba will support the idea of a girls' school and that he will talk to the imam about it. Juma and I reason that, since the Taliban no longer occupy our village, it should be easy to open a school for girls.

As soon as I get home, I tell Baba my idea. He agrees to speak to the imam, but he is not sure the imam will go along with it. I can tell my Baba likes the idea and has been thinking about it, because later at lunch, he tells me that he and I will go visit my teacher, and together they will go to the imam. This idea for a girls' school is a grand one indeed, Baba tells me, but it's also very risky. If we are successful, every girl's future will look brighter, as they will know how to read and write. We finish our lunch, then go to my teacher's house, where Baba shares with him our wish for a girls' school. My teacher agrees with Baba and decides to join him in speaking to the imam after evening prayer.

We stay with my teacher until prayers begin, talking about the village and the Taliban and the American soldiers—all the recent events. At the mosque after evening prayers, my Baba and teacher meet with the imam to present our idea. I will be so happy for my sisters if we can get them a school. After a while, Baba, my teacher, and the imam come out to where I am waiting. Baba is smiling as he approaches. He tells me the imam has agreed to ask the rest of the village if they want to have a girls' school, and has even offered to use an area of the mosque for this purpose. The imam tells us he will call out on the loudspeaker for all villagers to visit the mosque to discuss this grand idea.

We all agree that this will be the best course of action. As Baba and I walk home, I tell him how happy I am for my sisters, and how much better they will feel if they can also go to school. He seems to be as excited as I am, and now we just have to wait for the imam's call the next evening. My sisters are overjoyed when Baba and I tell them our plan. They cannot believe they may have the opportunity to attend school—to get educated—and we spend the entire dinner talking of nothing else.

The next day goes by slowly. After school I go home with Juma for lunch and then we distract ourselves by playing in the jungle at our favorite pastime of searching for birds' nests. Finally, evening comes and we hear the imam make the announcement over the loudspeaker for all villagers to go to the mosque. The mosque is filled with the people of the village, who listen intently as the imam speaks. He lectures the people on their responsibility to teach their children the right way, to which everyone nods and agrees. He next says that all children should go to school, regardless of if they are boys or girls. At this, the people are silent. They don't know what to do or say.

The imam looks around, then asks for the people who will let their daughters go to school to stand up. My Baba is the first person to stand up. No one else moves. The imam looks through the crowd again, and again, no one else stands. He asks if anyone can show him where, in The Holy Quran, it says that females are not allowed to receive an education. More silence. Finally, the imam says, "I know you think you can't let your daughters go to school because of the dangers of the Taliban, but if you men are Muslim and accept the teachings of the Quran, you know the Quran says that both males and females need to be educated. And, education is very important. If our people are not educated, they will not know about or understand the rights of all human beings."

The imam is passionate in his words, and angry at the lack of support, but eventually more people stand with my Baba. At first only thirteen men stand, but more join him slowly as the night wears on. By now it is time for the sunrise Fajr prayer, but the imam threatens the people who are not standing, telling them they will need to find a new imam and build their own mosque. I know the imam knows the people can't build a new mosque on their own, and this makes me smile. He is such a great man. After this, I am amazed at what happens next. Over half the people in the village stand to allow their daughters go to school. But, while some people are still not ready for this change, the imam says, "I am not worried about this decision from those who did not stand, because one day they will realize their error, and then they will let their daughters attend school."

This change is to happen immediately. Starting the next day, the girls' school will open. Baba and I are so happy with this outcome we can't wait to get home. I tell this to my sisters, and they are ecstatic. They can't wait to go to school, to prove they can do well too.

Because I pass the mosque on my way to school, I tell my sisters to walk with me the next morning. For once I will not be alone on my morning walk to school, as I will now walk with my sisters on their way to school. And we follow this routine happily every day. I drop them at the mosque and continue on to my own school.

After a half year of this, the imam decides that the small space he has set aside in the mosque is no longer sufficient to serve as the girls' school. Baba, my teacher, and the imam decide we should go to the American base in the Urgun District, to see if they will assist us in erecting a new school building. The imam and Baba want me to come with them, which makes me very proud, and we also have our village's consular, a government official, join us. The consular listens intently as Baba and the other adult men explain how important we believe it is for the girls of our village to have their own school. I say nothing, but just listen and watch them all as the conversation goes back and forth. I am, after all, a small boy, but proud to be present as Baba's eldest son.

When we arrive at the military base, Baba drives up to the security gate. We face an unexpected but familiar problem of trying to communicate, as we cannot speak English, and the Americans at the gate do not speak Pashto. As a result, they initially turn us away. I am surprised there is a problem at all, since we know so many of the soldiers. Thankfully the consular knows enough English to explain that we would like to build a school for our girls, so they can be educated like the boys. The soldiers cautiously eye our imam because of his full beard, which must make them think of the Taliban. Despite their wariness, however, they search us and allow us inside the base.

The adults are led into a separate room to speak with a representative of the United States Army. I am left in the hall with several soldiers, but that is no problem for me. I know them! They are the same ones who came to my village to hand out toys and candies, and so we play. In fact, they give me more toys and things to play with. Every soldier has his picture taken with me, but I am still unable to communicate with them. They keep talking to me, but I don't understand a word they say. Even so, I am having fun and feel totally safe with these men. I have nearly forgotten why I am there, and am half-confused when Baba comes out and calls me to go in with him. He tells me some soldiers want to ask me questions, since I am already a student in our village, but that first I am to speak with a translator in another room.

The translator asks me why the people of my village want to make a girls' school. I tell him, as honestly as possible, "The Quran says that it is our responsibility to make our children educated and let them go to school, whether they are boys or girls." He asks me just this one question, then asks where I learned this answer. "From our imam!" I say. "He taught us this."

The translator smiles, and indicates the soldiers can now join us. When they hear my response, they seem just as pleased as the translator. The soldiers tell the consular they will give us a signed letter with the official stamp of the base that we are to take to the governor of the Paktika Province. Baba, the imam, my teacher, and I are thrilled with the overwhelming success of our trip. We leave the base, and Baba drives the consular, my teacher, and the imam back to their homes, then we return home ourselves. Baba has another trip to make the next day—to Paktika Province to meet the governor about the school.

The next morning, Baba prepares to leave, and I hear him tell my mother that he is taking the imam and my teacher with him. The thought occurs to me and I jump on the idea. "Baba, if you are taking my teacher, school will be closed, right?"

"Yes, Hayat, I suppose school will be closed for the day."

"Can I go with you, then, since I will have no school?" Success! My logic is flawless, and Baba allows me to accompany him.

The road to Paktika Province is completely torn up and barely passable in areas. I have ridden on this road to Paktika Province from the Sarobi District many times, but the road was good then, and the trip usually takes just two hours. This time it takes us over five hours to make the drive, but we eventually arrive and meet with the governor. We ask him for approval for two new schools: one for girls and the other for boys. Baba produces the letter from the American soldiers, and hands it to the governor, who looks it over and agrees to the project. The governor gives us his own signed letter of approval, and tells us to take both letters to Kabul. We learn the governor's letter expresses urgency for the girls' school, since they have neither a teacher nor a proper school house now, other than the space at the mosque, and that he has also put in for a new, expanded school building for the boys.

The governor tells us to go to Kabul right away, since there will soon be elections and he is not sure what will happen after that. We decide to leave our car at the governor's estate and go by taxi to Kabul. Thankfully, this road is better, smoother, which makes this leg of our long day's journey easier.

We arrive in Kabul in the evening, and I can't believe my eyes. In just these past few years, Kabul has completely transformed. The last time I was here was with my Uncle Ibrahim to see Hamid Karzai after the Taliban government had been defeated. At that time, Kabul was nothing. Now I see buildings that are three and four stories tall—so high compared to the one-floor buildings I am used to—parks, and many other changes throughout the city. We no longer know our way to the Ministry of Education building. The taxi driver discovers the way, but when we arrive, we find the building is closed. We book a hotel for the night, not wanting to make the long trip back home. Another change in Kabul is that the price of a hotel room has doubled, but we find one and check in for the night. After dinner, we go to bed, knowing our plan first thing in the morning is to go to the Ministry of Education.

The next day we wake up early and after breakfast head straight to the Ministry of Education, where we meet with the Governor of

Education. This meeting also turns out to be a success. He tells us he will send an engineer and workers to build the girls' school, and that they must get started before the election which is just ten days away. The concern is that, if a new president is elected, we will have to start all over with the registration and permitting for the school. And if procedures become computerized, we will have even more difficulty because we don't have a computer. These handwritten documents are all we have, as up till now, business has been conducted verbally, on a handshake, and with an occasional agreement in writing. The governor also promises to pass our request for the boys' school on to the new government, saying that they will help us build a school with greater capacity for more classrooms and students. This pleases us all greatly. We thank him and start our trip back home.

We finally arrive back in our village two days later, where everyone is awaiting our news. The imam announces the good news at the mosque. He tells everyone that the government will be building a school for the girls, and that a new building for the boys will be coming soon. Many people cannot truly believe that this will happen, but I go to bed that night knowing we have done something incredible—something that will make life for my sisters better.

I am awakened the next morning by the imam's voice through the loudspeaker. He is calling everyone to the mosque. As we proceed to the mosque, we see American and Afghan soldiers, as well as Afghan police in our village. We pick up our pace, as we are anxious to see what is going on, and then realize they are present to oversee the people's registration for the upcoming election—the first in our history.

Everyone from our village stands in line for their registration cards. Half are in favor of the election and the other half are not. But the imam says we are to do this, and so we must, as no one can change what the imam says. The day turns out to be a long one, as the last registration card isn't handed out until after sunset. The adults are told they must present their cards on Election Day, noted with their choice for president. They will drop their cards into a voting box and the votes will then be counted. We really don't know who is running for President of Afghanistan, other than Hamid Karzai, but my parents will drop their cards in his box when the time comes.

After the Americans and Afghani police leave for their camps, the imam reminds everyone that the government will be building the girls' school over the next ten days, before the elections take place. Everyone is once again excited at the thought.

Ten days come and go, but no workers arrive in that time. The village waits patiently, but nothing happens. My family drops their election cards into Hamid Karzai's box, and the school remains unbuilt. What has happened in the days since our long trip to see the governor in Kabul?

Chapter Five
2004

It is October 9. We hear that Hamid Karzai has won the election, and he will be our president again. We prefer him to the Taliban, and I've seen how Kabul has improved under his leadership, so this makes us happy. Of course, there is much anger in the village, because the promised school building has not been started—no word from anybody, no signs that the project will ever get started. All we have are some signed papers, apparently meaningless in this big world. Coincidentally, my Baba's visa to travel to Dubai has expired, also for the sake of the school.

Because of the long wait and broken promise, Baba plans to travel back to Kabul to see the Minister of Education. But good fortune is with us, for just as we head out to tell the others in the village about Baba's plan, we see construction equipment and a group of workers gathered near the mosque talking with some of the villagers. Baba and I walk over to the group and introduce ourselves. They tell us that all the workers and engineers are here to build the school, but they are asking for security to protect them because they feel our province is too close to the Pakistan border and the Taliban could come to attack them. The imam turns to those of us gathered, and asks for volunteers to stand with the workers as security during construction. Many young people gladly pick up his call to keep the workers safe. Next the imam shows the engineer the location selected for building the school. It now seems work is set to begin the next day. Finally! The girls' school is going to be built!

This lifts the spirits of my entire village, and the imam asks if anyone can offer a sacrifice the next day at the masjid. He tells us that the sacrifice will be to thank the people who are building our school and show them appreciation for what they are doing. A few families, including my Baba, offer to bring what they can. Our contribution will be two goats. With that, everyone heads home to prepare for the big day. I know I am happy with these events, but my Baba seems even happier, for his daughters will soon be able to go to school.

The next morning, Baba goes to the market to buy the goats while my sisters and I leave for school. In all the excitement about the new school, I have fallen a bit behind in my studies. And school has been extra busy, as we prepare for our upcoming final exam. Fortunately, I was able to focus on my studies that day.

On my walk home from school with the other students, we see a lot of people congregated around the mosque. They are all busy preparing what they have sacrificed and serving lunch to anyone who asks for it. We go over and ask for lunch for ourselves. We are told to sit down and wait our turn in line, at which time someone will bring us our lunch. The entire area is busy with people coming and going, food being prepared, people eating and, best of all, workers who have commenced work on the school.

Final exams are the next day. Juma and I have once again prepared for the exam together, and we both finish without any problem. As usual, because I can write faster than anyone, I finish my exam first. I am once again happy and excited knowing we have three months of vacation ahead of us.

We decide to go to Juma's house, where we have lunch and then go off to play in the jungle. We have grown taller and stronger, and realize we can climb the trees that were once too big for us to reach. Climbing the trees is fun, because we can look out over the village from up high. After a while, though, we decide to go to the site where the new girls' school is being built. We are anxious to watch and understand the progress, and we bombard the workers with questions as our curiosity takes over. The men are friendly and they understand why we are so excited, but they tell us it will take one year to build the school. This is much longer than the ten days we were initially told, but I know how to handle a long time—it's like when Baba goes away to Dubai for work.

Juma and I remain at the worksite for a long while. When we realize it is late, we head home. Baba tells me he leaves for Pakistan in the morning so that he can send a copy of his passport to Dubai. He must do this in order to get a new visa. Even now, advanced telecommunications services and technology have not reached our village, so we, like most others, must still go to Pakistan if we have to send something urgent to Dubai or if we need to call Dubai. We must still do many things in person.

* * *

Our three-month school vacation passes quickly and Juma and I look forward to returning to school, for the next day is Results Day, when we get the results of our final exam. This year, Juma is in first position and I am in second. I know I finished second because I missed so many days this past year, but I'm happy because my friend has worked hard for his first-place position. At home, Baba is preparing to leave for Dubai in a few days. He has renewed his work visa, and must attend to his business.

While Baba is getting his things together and Mom is cooking dinner, my younger sister holds Sadiqullah in her lap, playing with him. Somehow, she drops my little brother on his head. I look first at my sister, then at Sadiqullah, who says nothing—he does not even cry. I run to tell my father what happened and that we need to take Sadiqullah to the doctor. Sadiqullah remained unconscious for twenty minutes. We are all extremely frightened and for a terrible moment think he is dead, but just then, he blinks and, thanks to Allah, we know at least that he is alive.

We quickly jump into the car and go to the doctor in the Urgun District. He gives Sadiqullah some medicine and injections which awaken him, and he starts crying. We are happy to see Sadiqullah apparently better, but the doctor tells us we must take him to Kabul or Peshawar in Pakistan for further testing, because his case is serious and requires additional treatment. Baba and Mom agree, and say they will take Sadiqullah to Kabul in the morning. In Kabul, Sadiqullah is checked by a doctor, but the doctor does not have modern technology such as a CT scan. He tells my parents to never leave Sadiqullah alone, to keep watch over him, because his injury is internal and he could possibly go into a coma.

While Baba and Mom are away in Kabul, my aunt comes to our house to help my sisters with the cooking and the house work. For three days, my sisters miss school and we are left to wonder what is happening with our little brother. When our parents return from Kabul, Sadiqullah is better. Obviously, Sadiqullah's situation is very dangerous, so we now make sure someone is with him at all times.

Baba is finally ready to leave for Dubai. Thankfully it is for only one month, and not the one or two years like he has done in the past. Uncle Marjan and I make the well-worn journey with Baba to the Sarobi

District, where he will begin his trip via taxi to Angor Adah, then to Wanah, in Waziristan Province, Pakistan, then to Dubai.

With the months that have passed, the girls' school is almost completed, and just a little work remains. The workers tell us it will be finished in one or two months. Juma and I are busy fourth-year students. We study together every day, and I am much better in my attendance, as I don't have to miss any school days this year. While I am glad my best friend Juma was in the first position at the start of this year, I plan to regain my first-place position by the end of the school year—of that I am confident.

Chapter Six
2005

In just one short month, so many exciting things have happened. My Baba returned from Dubai and the girls' school is finally completed. In fact, just one day remains for the grand opening of the school. Teachers—all men—have come from other provinces to teach at this new school. Baba, the imam, and my teacher Naseeb Khan are busy working on their plans to celebrate the opening of the school.

The imam invites all the villagers to the masjid and asks everyone to donate one thousand rupees (approximately ten U.S. dollars) to go toward the school's opening day celebration. The people agree and pay their money. The imam counted 140,000 rupees from everyone's donations—money we will use to buy a big cow to sacrifice, fresh fruit, and everything else we need for the celebration. Baba, my teacher, the imam, and several others go off to purchase all the food and supplies. Everyone is busy running around and preparing for the school opening, so Juma and I decided to take a walk around the girls' school. Everything is so new and beautiful. We just love all the classrooms and hope the boys have a similar beautiful school someday. When we finish at the school, Juma goes home, as do I to wait for Baba to return. When Baba finally arrives, I see he doesn't have a cow.

"Where is the cow, Baba?" I ask.

"The cow is at your teacher's house," he says. "Now, let us have dinner so we can get to bed early. Tomorrow morning we have lots of work to do for the celebration."

* * *

The whole family gets up early the next morning. As soon as we finish breakfast, we head to the girls' school, where so many others from the village have already gathered. The first order of the day is to sacrifice the cow and prepare it to be cooked. Everyone at the school is busy and hard at work finalizing things for the celebration until twelve o'clock in afternoon.

At last, everything is ready and people have come from other surrounding villages to join in the celebration. The imam invites everyone to enter the school where the food will be served. Lunch continues until four o'clock, after which the engineer speaks to the crowd. He explains that the school has twelve classrooms and each will have a teacher. He next introduces the teachers. Everyone is ecstatic to hear the girls will have twelve teachers.

Juma and I look at each other. We are incredulous at this news, and Juma whispers, "We still have only two teachers and a school that too small! The girls are lucky."

The celebration ends after all the announcements have been made and everybody begins to wander home. Juma and I, however, are still remembering how lucky the girls are with their new school, and so have devised a plan. On our way home, I tell my Baba he needs to go back to the Ministry of Education in Kabul to request a new boys' school because we want a new school like the girls have.

Baba doesn't think long before agreeing with our request. But he tells me he wants to first ask the imam and my teacher if they would be willing to go back. If they agree, then Baba says he would go back to Kabul whenever they are ready.

The next morning, I get ready to go school with my sisters, and Baba goes to see the imam and my teacher to discuss the possibility of going back to Kabul.

Juma and I are now supposed to have English classes. As a result of the U.S. occupation, our president Hamid Karzai decided English would be taught in our schools. This makes me very happy because I already know some words in English. The problem is that very few people in our country know English well enough to teach it. Because of this, there is no teacher for my school. When I find out we will not have English classes after all, I am disappointed. We have a science class instead. By 11:30, our school day has ended, and Juma and I walk home, separating at the usual spot along the way. At home, my sisters are waiting to have lunch with me, but I have other plans.

"You go ahead and eat. I'm not too hungry yet and want to eat with Baba," I tell my sisters.

But they force the issue by saying, "Hayat, if you don't eat, we won't eat either."

I relent and go to wash my hands. Just then, Baba arrives, so now we all sit down and eat together.

"Baba, did you meet with the imam and my teacher?"

"Yes, Hayat. We have spoken, and tomorrow we will go to Kabul."

This makes me happy, so I quickly finish my lunch and head to Juma's to tell him the good news. We go out to the jungle to climb trees. The trees are tall, but Juma and I have grown over the past five years and now climb them easily. From up in the trees, we talk and laugh and watch the many birds that inhabit the jungle. Then I recall a distant memory.

"Juma, let's go to the nest that we saw the first time we played together in the jungle five years ago!" Juma likes that idea, and so we locate the very same tree and climb it. To our surprise, we realize our hands are too big to fit inside the hole where the nest was. We look at each other and burst out laughing.

"No more birds' nests for us!" I say, and we climb down from the tree and run off to play in other parts of the jungle. That afternoon we enjoy one of our best times ever playing together in the jungle.

When I realize how late it is, I return home, where I help my sisters with their Pashto lessons. Baba soon returns from the mosque and we sit down to dinner. He tells us about his plans for his trip to Kabul the next day. He then says, "Tomorrow morning I must wake up early for my trip, so let's finish dinner and go to bed."

* * *

"Come back quickly, my husband," says Mom. "I don't know how much longer this baby will wait to be born."

"I know," says Baba. "I will be back as soon as our work there is done. I want to be here with you to welcome our new son or daughter to this world."

Baba leaves for Kabul and my sisters and I leave for school. This continues for twelve days, and we are without any news from Baba, the imam, or my teacher. On the thirteenth day, Mom tells my sisters and me that she needs to go to the doctor's, but this is a problem because our car is not home. I remind her that we don't have a car and tell her to wait just one more day. "If Baba comes home today, he will take you. If he does not return today, tomorrow I will tell my uncle to pick us up and take us to the doctor's."

Mom agrees to this plan, but it is now evening and I see she is in a lot of pain. I am very sad for her, even though she does not complain aloud to us. I just look at her face and see how much pain she is in. We now have no choice but to go to the doctor's without Baba. Amazingly, just then I hear the sound of our car and go out to see Baba has returned home. I'm very happy he always manages to come home at just the right time.

This time he is not alone. He has brought with him the map engineer and workers for the boys' school, and tells me to get dinner ready for twenty people! I immediately tell Sobia to start cooking, but then tell Baba he needs to help Mom. "She is in too much pain and can't wait any longer, Baba. She needs to get to the doctor's now."

Baba goes inside to see Mom and asks her if she can wait. She says no. Baba agrees it is time to go to the doctor's, but I'm worried that it is night and the doctor will be closed. Baba assures us that in the Urgun District there is a hospital that is open 24 hours. He prepares Mom for the trip and asks me to take care of the workers, the imam, and my teacher. Baba leaves for the hospital with Uncle Marjan and one of my younger sisters.

I have a lot to do! I return to our guests and after a time my sisters knock on the door and tell me dinner is ready. Men and women are separated in social situations, and when the imam is present, he speaks on only the men's side. The women can hear everything the imam says as well as the discussion among the men, but the women are not allowed to participate in the conversation. I ask our guests to wash their hands while I take dinner out to them. Once everyone is seated and eating, the imam asks me where my father is. I explain that he had to take my mother to the doctor.

When everyone has finished eating, I offer tea, but they say they are ready to leave. The imam tells the workers to go with him. "For tonight, you will sleep in the same place where the workers for the girls' school slept." He adds, "In the morning we will locate a different place for you to sleep that will be near the boys' school."

Everyone leaves and my sisters and I wait for Baba and Mom to return home. That night, our little brother Sadiqullah is the only one who gets a good night's sleep.

It is midnight when they return from the hospital, along with our new baby brother! Baba gets out of the car and is so happy to tell me we have a new brother in the family. Now we are three brothers and three sisters! I note that my new brother has been born during the autumn months, because leaves are falling from the trees. In my country, we don't live by months and days as people in other countries do, but rather by the season. In fact, we do not note individual dates such as birthdays and do not have birth certificates that document when a person is born. I do not even know the exact date of my own birth.

But we are happy and I tell Baba I will come up with a name for my new baby brother just as I did with Sadiqullah. Baba tells me has already chosen the name for him—Najeebullah. Mom comes inside and we are very happy to see she is well and that our family has grown by one. But it is late and everyone is tired, especially Mom. My oldest sister will take care of her till morning. I go to bed happy that night. Me, my Baba, and my two other sisters sleep in the room where Sadiqullah is already asleep, and my mom and older sister sleep in a different room with Najeebullah nearby.

We get up early the next morning because of our excitement for our new baby brother and all the work ahead. My sister prepares breakfast for everyone and Baba gets ready to go to the market for goats. Our plan is to have a party like the one we had when Sadiqullah was born. Baba leaves for the market and I follow him out and head toward my school so I can see the workers who are building our new boys' school.

When I arrive at school I look everywhere for Juma to tell him my big news. When I find him, I nearly explode. "Juma, I have a new baby brother!"

Juma recalls the celebration we had when Sadiqullah was born just two years earlier, and hopes we have another grand celebration. "Are you having a party like before?"

"Yes, tomorrow night," I tell him.

Even though we are at the school, we don't have any classes. Juma and I and some others have just come to see the workers. They are busy making a sleeping room for themselves, so we decide to leave. On the way back home I ask Juma to come home with me but he says he will come to the party the next day.

By now Baba is also back from the market. This time he brings six goats for sacrificing.

"Baba, four goats are enough," I say. "Why did you bring six?"

"Hayat, two are for the school sacrifice and four are for our party."

"Oh." I nod my head and think about all the fun we will have the next day with the sacrifice at my school during the day and then the party at our home at night with the other sacrificing.

After lunch, I ask Baba if we can take the goats to our farm land. When he agrees, I race out to Juma's to tell him about the six goats. "Juma! We have six goats to play with until tomorrow!" Juma is just as excited as I am, and together we run back to my house. We take the goats out to the field and let them eat. They all like the apples. We don't stop them from eating too much because we know they will be sacrificed the next day. At five o'clock we lead the goats back home from the field.

I ask Juma, "Why don't you stay at my house tonight because tomorrow morning we have to do the sacrifice here and at the boys' school?" Juma agrees, and we eat dinner and then go to bed. We fall asleep quickly because we know we will have lots of work to do in the morning.

We awake early and my sister brings us breakfast. When we finish, we go and invite some of our neighbors to help with the sacrifice of the goats. Baba asks me to take two goats to the boys' school to sacrifice there. Juma and I round up two of the goats and head to the school. Many of the villagers are already there, so we leave the goats with them to sacrifice and cook for lunch.

We want to hurry back home for the sacrificing of the goats for our party that night, but Baba and one of our neighbors has already sacrificed the goats and the cooking has begun. At lunch time, most everyone in the village goes to the school to have the sacrifice lunch there, but we are very busy with our own preparations so we stay home to continue our work. After all, that night is our party! We build the two halls again—one for the women and the other for the men—and they are finally ready.

The guests arrive and we serve everyone dinner. As people finish eating, I hear some of them ask for the tape player so we can get the music started. That's good news! We get to listen to music on the tape player again! I can't believe my eyes when I see what Baba does. He surprises everyone. He brings out a big tape player with large loudspeakers! The music plays loudly and the men dance a *meli attan*, a traditional dance of Afghanistan. The party and celebration continues until midnight, when people begin to leave for home. Juma and I are exhausted and fall asleep in minutes. The next morning, I can barely open my eyes and wonder how I can possibly go to school that day. The next thing I know, it is eleven o'clock and Juma and I have missed school!

We have our breakfast and then go to the jungle to play in the trees. We love the jungle and are always quite comfortable playing there. Like so many other times in the jungle, the day flies by and we don't even notice when it gets late. But eventually we know it is time to go back home, so Juma goes his way and I go mine.

When I arrive, I find my sisters staring at my little brother Sadiqullah as he sleeps. But they have strange looks on their faces, so I ask them what they are doing. I quickly realize the situation is serious. My sisters are unable to wake Sadiqullah. We drip some water on him, but he doesn't move at all. My sisters start to cry, but I tell them to calm down. "I have to think," I tell them. "Okay. I must tell Baba that Sadiqullah is in a coma. The doctor told us once before to never leave him alone. You stay here and I will go find Baba." I run to the mosque and tell Baba that Sadiqullah is in a coma. Together we run back home. By the time we arrive, my mother is with Sadiqullah and everyone is crying. My Baba places his hand over Sadiqullah's heart and tells us he is alive. "We must go quickly to the hospital in Urgun."

We finally arrive at the hospital and it is very late, but there are doctors present to help us. The doctors tell us we must take Sadiqullah to the hospital on the American base in Urgun, which is about a twenty-five-minute drive. We are given permission to go to the base and tell the guard that we have an emergency, and the guard will then allow us entry into the base hospital. So, we get back in the car and drive as quickly as we can to the American hospital. At the gates, the soldiers shine high-powered flashlights at us. The lights are so bright we can't even see the road. My Baba stops the car and calls out to the soldiers for help. "My son is very ill. We have an emergency appointment." The guards shut off the lights and allow us entry onto the Urgun base.

As soon as the soldiers see Sadiqullah they take him from Baba. "Your son needs oxygen. Follow us," they say through their translator. We also learn Sadiqullah's heartbeat is zero. We run behind the Americans soldiers into their hospital room where they put an oxygen mask over Sadiqullah's mouth. They tell us they don't have the best doctors at this camp and that they want to take us by helicopter to Kabul-Bagram, which is a larger base with a better-equipped hospital—the same hospital where they treat wounded American soldiers. I hear them explain, "The big bases have the best doctors."

In under five minutes they have started two helicopters for us—one that takes Sadiqullah and the soldiers who keep the oxygen on him, and the second for Baba and me. The wind from the helicopter rotors almost blows my cap off as I try to get in the helicopter, but I finally make it inside. This is my first time ever in a helicopter. In fact, the only times I have been up in the air at all are when I am in the trees with Juma. I'm frightened at the thought of flying, but the soldier next to me fastens my seat belt and suddenly I feel fine. The soldiers give us headphones to cover our ears.

The translator tells us the wind is too strong to land in Kabul, and that we must go to Khost, which is another forty-five minutes away. "Okay," my father says. When we finally land, the doctors are already waiting for us. They take Sadiqullah to the operating room, where he is still in a coma and saying nothing. The hospital gives Baba and me a room near Sadiqullah. We can't see him, but at least we are in the hospital with him. By now his heart beat is at one percent. I pray to Allah to save Sadiqullah's life.

The bring us dinner but we are not hungry. The cook thinks we are not eating because we think the food is not halal, that is, prepared according to our custom, but she misunderstands. We are simply not hungry. The cook picks up a plate and says, "This is chicken." But we don't know English, so she sets the plate down and makes sounds like a chicken. My Baba laughs at her, and then I laugh too, but she gets angry and calls in the translator. The translator explains the food is halal and fine to eat, but we tell him we aren't worried about the food not being halal—we are just too tired and not hungry. The translator tells the cook we simply are not hungry, and she tells him she will leave the food with us in case we get hungry later. By now it is midnight and we are still waiting for news about Sadiqullah but none comes. Eventually we fall asleep.

Morning comes and the same woman brings us breakfast. This time we eat because we are hungry. She removes the chicken meal from the previous night, and I hear her laugh a bit as she leaves our room. By noon we still have heard no news about Sadiqullah. We have no choice but to wait quietly. The doctors are trying their best to save him.

That afternoon they perform a spinal tap to check Sadiqullah's spinal fluid. Later the doctors tell us that he finally cried and opened his eyes. Of course he saw only the doctors and asked for our Mom. But Mom is home with my baby brother. I am allowed to go into the operating room so Sadiqullah can see me. All I can think about is how many scars he will have. But I learn the doctors didn't cut open his back. They only had to use a needle to remove the fluid. When I go into the room Sadiqullah looks at me. He can hardly talk and I am crying, but the doctors tell me not to cry because my little brother is saved. I go to the bed and kiss him. My Baba enters the room now, and through the translator, the doctors tell him that we will stay at the base for three days.

We settled in for our three days and felt much better. I wished we could share the good news with my mom and sisters, but there are still no phones in my village.

At last the doctors tell us they will release Sadiqullah to us within two hours. My brother is very cute and the soldiers are busy playing with him and giving him a lot of toys.

When it is finally time to leave, we take a rental car to the Urgun District. The road there from the base is in horrible condition—all broken up and full of potholes. Our helicopter trip to the base was so different by comparison. We reach Urgun by sunset and go to the base where we had left our own car days earlier. We still have another drive of more than thirty minutes to get home. The soldiers at the gate look at

Sadiqullah and see he is awake and talking. My brother's improvements make them smile. We start the car and head home, finally. My mom and sisters are waiting at the door as we pull the car up to the house. Their eyes are red because they were sad and crying for three full days with no news about any of us. But when they see Sadiqullah with us and that he is walking and talking, they are very happy. They cry again, but this time their tears are for happiness.

Sadiqullah is only two years old but very smart. The woman who fed him at the base was a black American woman, and my brother kept saying "mama" over and over the whole time he was there. Sadiqullah runs to our mom now because he was away from her for five days. But now we are finally together again, sitting in our own home and watching Sadiqullah play with toys he got from the American base.

Baba says to Mom, "The American doctors gave us a letter and told us to buy the same injection and bottles and drugs for Sadiqullah for the next three years. We will buy all of this in Peshawar, Pakistan, but you know it is a long trip to get there." Now that Sadiqullah is better, it seems we are all going to school the next day.

* * *

My sisters and I go to school every day. And every day we see the progress on the new boys' school, which is now close to completion. Some work remains, but it should be completed in just a few days. We are very happy to see the great progress that is being made.

Exams start in three days, so we are all spending a lot of time studying and getting ready for them, especially me. Last school year I was in second position, but this time I want to regain my first-place position. These final three days I do not go anywhere. I just stay home and keep reading and reviewing all my study books and answers so I will be as ready as I possibly can for my exam.

On exam day, Juma and I walk to school together. The teacher arrives and hands out the question papers. I get right to work. I work through all the questions and am first to hand my paper in to the teacher. Outside I wait for Juma, as I am going home with him. When he finishes, he comes out and we are happy to start another three months of vacation. Before we leave, however, our teacher tells me to wait for him because he wants to tell me something. When the teacher finishes inside, he comes out and talks to Juma and me. He announces that he wants us to study in the higher, more advanced classes.

Juma and I look at each other and both have the same question for him. "How can we move up to the advanced classes? We still need to learn the materials in the previous classes."

But our teacher has a plan for us. He says, "I spoke with one of the teachers in the girls' school, Abdul Wahab. He teaches advanced classes and has agreed to teach the subjects from grade levels seven to nine during this year's school vacation."

This seems very hard. How can we learn three grade levels of information in only three months? I tell our teacher, "We will go home and think about it."

Back at home I tell Baba what the teacher wants Juma and me to do. He says, "Hayat, it will be very hard to do all of this in three months. Why don't you just study one subject this vacation, like English?"

"Baba, I think I can do that! I will go to my teacher's home later this afternoon."

When I tell my teacher my new plan, he is also happy for me to learn English, and together we go to see the teacher at the girls' school. We all agree on the study plan, but I am expected to gather more boys to learn English this vacation. This way, we will be able to pay the teacher for his extra work. Then I go with my teacher to speak with the imam about opening an English class for the students in the village. The imam is also happy about this and tells us that after prayer he will invite everyone who wants their children to learn English.

That evening, the imam talks about Abdul Wahab's English course for the students in the village and explains that the monthly bill will be five hundred rupees (approximately five dollars). Twenty-three students from our school are ready to join the class, but Juma is not present. I add him to make it twenty-four.

Class starts the next day, and I am so busy thinking about learning English that I forget to tell Juma. He is not at the first class. Although we do not really learn anything yet, because the teacher just takes the time to tell us what we need to know about the class. He tells us to buy

English notebooks and an English grammar book. He also tells us that class will start at nine o'clock in the morning and go for two and a half hours. Back at home I ask Baba to get English grammar books and English notebooks for me and for Juma. Baba leaves for the shops and I race to Juma's to tell him the big news. His mother feeds us lunch and we run out to the jungle to play for the afternoon. I really love to visit Juma's because it is in the jungle and I never grow tired of seeing all different kinds of trees and birds. I also love to see the mountains that stand directly behind his home. For me, Juma lives in a perfect place.

I tell Juma to go home with me that night and the next day we can go to English class together. We ask his parents' permission and they agree. Back at my house, Juma asks to see my little brother Najeebullah. I ask Mom if she will bring Najeebullah out for us to see. She does, but he is very small, so there is not much we can do with him. Sadiqullah, however, is at a fun age. He is really cute and is learning a few new words every day. Juma and I spend time talking with my little brother. He makes us laugh. After a while my Baba returns with our English books and notebooks. Juma is happy when he sees my father also bought a notebook and English grammar book for him.

Evening comes, and Juma and I talk about the next day and then spend some time looking at our English books. We don't understand a thing! After dinner, Baba tells Mom that he is going to go to his aunt's house, and Juma and I are ready to sleep because we have to be ready for class by nine a.m. the next day.

* * *

The first day of English class, our teacher teaches us the A-B-Cs. We write in our notebooks and the teacher tells us to learn all the letters from A to Z by the next day. Juma and I smile because we already know the alphabet. We learned it from the American soldiers. Class goes until 11:30 and then we all go home.

Baba is home and I ask him why he went to his aunt's house the night before. Baba looks at Mom, who already knows why, then he tells us that his aunt is asking for Sobia's hand in marriage for her son Aqal Khan. Baba agreed.

At this news, I decide to go to my older sister to see if she is happy with this marriage. "Do you know Baba visited his aunt last night, and that she asked for your hand in marriage to her son Aqal Khan?"

When she hears this, she starts crying. She asks me to tell Baba that she doesn't want to marry. She wants only to stay in this house with us and Mom and Baba.

I tell her, "Sobia, you are silly. Everyone has to get married."

I go to my parents' room tell them my sister is crying because she doesn't want to marry.

My mom tells me every girl goes through this drama. "Hayat, I did this when your grandmother asked for my hand in marriage to your father. It's drama." I let the subject drop, but during lunch Mom and Baba talk about his aunt who will visit our house the next day to fix the date for asking for my sister's hand. All I see is one very unhappy person, my sister Sobia. Mom tells me that on the inside my sister is happy, and the outside we just see all her drama. I believe Mom, and head out with Baba to go to the mosque before dinner.

* * *

The next morning, I leave home for my walk to English class. The teacher starts class every day promptly at nine. But it is wintertime and very cold, so I wear a big jacket to stay warm. Once in school, I hand in my homework. That day we learn about nouns. I notice that Juma doesn't understand and he did not do his homework. I wonder if he doesn't want to learn and I'm forcing him to take this class? Perhaps tomorrow will be a better day for him. When class ends, we each return home.

I see that my father's aunt and her son are at my house. They are talking with Baba and Mom about the date for my sister's engagement, so I take my lunch to my room to eat. But before I leave, I hear them say the engagement will be the next day! I can't believe it! Does Sobia know this?

Baba is going to get one or more goats to sacrifice for this occasion. He also he needs to buy outfits for fifty men and dresses for twenty women, as is the custom. At the time of an engagement, there are always many more men involved than women. And those women who do participate are the older women, those over forty. All these clothes are for the people that will be coming to our home with my father's aunt for the engagement event. Baba goes to the market and picks up all the goods that will be needed for the engagement celebration. Baba's aunt leaves, as she needs to go back to her home to invite her family and friends.

Engagements and marriage in Afghanistan, especially in our province of Paktika, have some very unique traditions, much involving a lot of back and forth between the families. First, the parents of the boy and girl meet and ask each other to establish a relationship between the families. Then the boy's family has to go to the girl's family to ask for the girl's hand for their son. The boy's parents then go to the girl's home to meet the girl. Then the girl's parents go to the boy's home to meet the boy. Each of the two families must decide if they want to form this relationship. When they agree on establishing the relationship, the girl's family performs a sacrifice, typically of a goat, and the boy's family visits the girl's home with upwards of fifty to seventy people, at which time the boy's family asks for the girl's hand in marriage.

At the same time, the boy's family understands they will have to pay the girl's family 500,000 to 1,200,000 Pakistan rupees (approximately $5,000 to $11,500) on the wedding day. On the actual engagement day, they will have to pay up to 100,000 rupees ($1,000), but this type of extreme payment is absolutely forbidden in Islam because that makes the marriage arrangement appear more like a business. Some families make the payment. However, the bride's family does not usually accept the money. This old-world tradition combines with Islam, and the imam always tells people that this money exchange is forbidden. Such exorbitance is considered *haram*, which means it is against God's wishes, similar to drinking alcohol or eating pork. Although, a *mahar*—dowry—is allowed. One more thing—the boy will not meet the girl until the day they get married. They cannot even meet each other when the engagement happens. For a bride and groom to meet before the day of their wedding is also forbidden in Islam, but our people follow these customs because of our old, old culture. I think our culture is still one hundred years behind the rest of the world, maybe more.

Our people spend lots of money on engagements, but it is really spent for nothing other than food. Islam's ancient traditions and culture require everyone to get married. If you don't get married, people laugh at you and make fun of you. But some people are uneducated or poor and don't have enough money for these traditions. You know what happens then? They leave Afghanistan and go to other countries to find work so they can earn money for their marriage. Most go to Europe or countries in the Middle East such as Dubai, Qatar, or Saudi. These marriage traditions even cause some to lose their life because they try to get away by smuggling their way to Europe or the Middle East. Smuggling may be the cheaper way to escape, and many reach their objective by doing this, but many more are gone forever, that is, they lose their lives for the sake of marriage.

But this is not a problem for us and that day we are waiting for Baba to return with two goats and everything else we need for the engagement announcement celebration.

* * *

My family gets up early the next morning to begin preparations that include sacrificing the goats and cooking. I go to my English class and see that Juma did not come to class that day. I am worried about him. When class ends, I know I must get home even though I want to go see Juma. There is still much work to do for all the guests who will be coming to our house that evening for the engagement event. My mom has been busy all morning cooking all different kinds of food. But now she gets me lunch and I sit down to eat with my sisters. Afterwards, we all get back to work preparing all the food and everything else for our guests.

At last, evening has arrived! The guests show up at our house accompanied by the imam from our mosque. We take the women to their room and the men to theirs. The imam stands and prepares to speak. Although he addresses the men and speaks in their room, the women can hear everything he says. He talks about the relationship between men and women. He tells the guests about the money the boy's parents have to pay my parents and reminds us that, other than a modest dowry, paying large sums of money to a bride's family is forbidden in Islam.

Next the parents of Aqal Khan, my sister's intended husband, ask my parents for my sister's hand for their son for 700,000 rupees. My Baba accepts. At that point, Aqal Khan's parents pay us 100,000 rupees in cash. Baba accepts the money, but will immediately give this money back to Aqal Khan's parents. He returns 50,000 rupees on behalf of the imam, which is a show of respect performed by the people of the Afghani culture. Next Baba returns the other 50,000 rupees to Aqal Khan's parents on behalf of the guests. Everyone is happy because Baba has not taken any money for the engagement. They all hug each other and congratulate both my and Aqal Khan's families.

The next thing that happens is for the parents to set a wedding date. Aqal Khan's family request a date for the wedding and Baba says, "The wedding will be in five months. We have much to prepare!" Aqal Khan's family accepts this date, and the celebration comes to a close. All the guests leave, but everyone knows Aqal Khan's parents will soon be having a party in their home.

It is late and I am tired, but after everyone is gone, I go to Sobia's room to see how she is. She is crying again, only this time she does not make me sad because I know she is just being overly dramatic, like Mom said. On the inside, I know she is happy. I go back to my own room and go to bed. I have school in the morning and can't worry about Sobia's drama anymore that night.

The next morning, I see that Juma once again is not in school. I do not understand why. We both love school, and we were both excited when our teacher invited us to skip to the higher classes. I decide to go see him at his home right after school.

When I arrive, Juma opens the door and I ask him, "Juma, why are you home? Why don't you come to school with me?"

"Hayat, English is too hard for me."

I am shocked and saddened by Juma's response, and certain his decision to stop coming to class was a difficult one. I can't imagine school without Juma. And how will I study for the exam without him? But I accept his decision and tell him it is okay if he doesn't want to come. Everything between us is good again, and he asks his mom to bring us lunch. We eat our lunch and then walk to my house where we play on the farm. After playing outside all afternoon, Juma goes home, as do I. I have English class again in the morning, and must accept that I will continue my English classes alone, without Juma, for three months.

Chapter Seven
2006

The day for the grand opening of our new school has finally arrived, and we cannot be happier. Our new school will have twelve classrooms and eighteen teachers!

I am so excited as I walk to school that morning. From the distance, I see a group of American soldiers outside the school. I wonder what is going on, so I run the rest of the way to school. Imagine my surprise when I get there to see that nothing bad has happened. In fact, it is good news. The Americans of the International Security Assistance Force (ISAF) have come for the opening of our new school, and they have brought us new books, notebooks, pens, and school bags. They have brought us everything we need! The new teachers are with them, and together they open the school. They tell us the boys' school was built by ISAF. My old teacher Naseeb Khan tells all the students to stand in line and thank the ISAF. In unison we say, "Thank you, ISAF soldiers, for the beautiful school."

The ISAF soldiers take pictures as they hand out school supplies to the students and teachers. At noon, they go to the girls' school and hand out the same new school supplies to them. By two o'clock the ceremony is over. The ISAF soldiers go back to Urgun and all the students leave school for the day. We are so thankful for the help provided by the ISAF.

My sisters and I are now back at home. We all have our new supplies and say over and over again how thankful we are to the ISAF.

My mom reminds me what my teacher told me five years earlier, "Hayat, if you study, one day we will have the same government as America, with your help." I am happy to hear her tell me that, because I love my school and I love going to school more than anything. We have very good teachers, and can now study two and three subjects in a single day. In our old school, we only studied one subject a day because we had only one teacher, but now with eighteen, we can study much more every day. And before, we used to sit on the floor. But now we have desks and chairs!

* * *

Sobia's wedding is now just five days away. I previously told you how engagements work in our Paktika Province. I will now tell you about weddings. First, the groom's family must make the payment they promised the bride's family on the day of the engagement announcement. They bring this money the day before the wedding.

The wedding ceremony itself lasts two days. On the first day, the bride's family sacrifices a cow and cooks for at least five to six hundred people. The groom's family arrives at the bride's home with all their guests to enjoy the feast. After that, everyone goes to the groom's home. That night, the bride's family sacrifices a goat for the groom, and he then goes to the bride's house with at least thirty people, his friends. This is his first visit to the bride's home. The bride's brother provides the groom with new clothes that include the knee-length shirt and trousers, shoes, a cap, and a new watch, and the groom gets dressed in his new attire. The bride's parents also give the groom a new car as well as new outfits to each of the groom's guests. Next the groom and his guests enjoy dinner, and then the groom returns to his own home. This is only the first day!

On the second day, it is the groom's family's turn to sacrifice a cow and cook for some five hundred people. The guests all return to the bride's home, but this time the groom accompanies them. They get the bride and take her to the groom's home where the groom's family feeds all the guests. The bride's parents do not go with their daughter, but the bride's sister can accompany her. At this point, there has not yet been one time that both families, including the bride and groom, have been together.

Today is the day the groom's family is to bring the money to my family. We have already sacrificed a goat. The groom's family arrives with our imam and some other people. They give us the money, and Baba takes the money to his room and leaves it there.

We serve lunch to our guests, but no one touches their food, even though Baba has asked everyone to start eating. The imam tells my father to discount the amount of money the groom's family has paid, but Baba says no. We insist that everyone eat, and they do. Once they are finished, everyone leaves. Baba has asked the imam to stay behind, and he agrees. My father tells the imam he is not going to return a single rupee to the groom's family that day, but will give the money back on the wedding day. Our imam is happy to hear this.

Baba next heads out to the market to buy a cow to sacrifice for the wedding that is to occur the next day. When he returns home, he says we are to sacrifice the cow that very night, since the groom's family will arrive at noon the next day and we still have so much to prepare. In fact, we are up working all night, but by morning, everything is ready.

At noon, the groom's family and their guests arrive. We expect 500 people, but 374 arrive, and we start serving the food. Once everyone finishes their meal, they leave and return to the groom's home. By night time, the groom and his friends come to our home. I take him the clothes he is to wear, and he puts them on over his own clothes. After that, he sits down to eat with his friends, and my parents hand him the key to the car our family is giving him. Next, we give all the groom's friends their new clothes. The groom and his friends now have all they are to receive from us and they return to the groom's home. That night we all fall into bed completely exhausted.

The next morning, we wait for the groom's family to arrive and take my sister with them back to the groom's home. Soon enough, they all arrive and everyone is very excited. At that time, Baba gives all the money the groom's family had paid earlier back to the groom. Baba had no intention of keeping the money the groom's family had paid, but he accepted it initially as a gesture to show that his daughter is valuable; she is not free, and she is worth the money they paid. The groom's family is, of course, very happy that Baba returned their money. They leave with Sobia to return to the groom's home. Accompanying the bride are my two younger sisters and two of our neighbor's girls. They will remain with Sobia for three days and then return home. But the groom has not yet met the bride, and will not meet her during these three days, until after the imam registers their *nikah*, or marriage. After that, they will be able to meet.

Sobia is now a married woman! I have school the next day and so I want to prepare for school and then go to bed early.

* * *

School continues another two or three months, and the time for the final exam is fast approaching. One day in particular, August 2, I am on my way to school with my sister. I drop her off at her school and continue on to mine. When I arrive, I hear everyone talking about a Taliban warning. I find Juma and ask him what is going on. Juma tells me the Taliban sent letters to both the boys' and girls' schools warning them to close. The letters also stated that if the schools did not close, the Taliban would come and throw acid on the students' faces.

I hear this news and get scared, recalling this same feeling from many months before. Everyone is talking about this and everyone is scared. I have fear in my heart, but in my mind, I know we have to come to school because we have exams in just a few days. At 11:30 everyone leaves school and goes back home. We are all worried about what will happen. My sisters are also home and they say the Taliban sent a letter to their school saying the school must close. I share my story, and together we are all sad because we all love to go to school. I believe the Taliban are warning everyone and trying to scare us all. We sit down to eat and talk about our schools and the situation.

I say, "We should not be scared of the Taliban. We have to go to school every day until we have our exams."

We spend the afternoon quietly thinking and worrying. Even by dinner time I am not hungry. All I can do is think about school. But the next morning—and the next and the next after that—my sisters and I go to school. We have our exams in two days. We made it to the last day of school with no word from the Taliban. The night before exams, my sisters and I are up all night reviewing all our books. We also take time to pray for safety at school the next day.

* * *

The next morning, we leave home at our usual time to head to school. As we get closer, we realize the Taliban are there. They have kidnapped seven teachers from the girls' school and left a note hanging for us to see. The note says, "If we see any school open tomorrow, we will kidnap the students and behead them." Upon reading the note, fear enters our hearts and we all run back home immediately.

My mom sees us all race through the front door. With a worried look, she asks, "Why are you not in school?"

We explain that the Taliban kidnapped seven teachers from the girls' school and left notes at the entrance to both schools warning us to close everything down. My mother gets very frightened upon hearing this, as the Taliban are more dangerous than ever. Now they behead people like they would an animal.

I want to go into the village to find out what is going on, but am not allowed to go alone. Baba has finally returned home. He says everyone is talking about the Taliban. I beg him to do something about the kidnapped teachers. He says he cannot do a thing because the Taliban have no court and no jail—they are lawless—and he would not know where to go. He says that once the Taliban have kidnapped someone, that means they will kill that person. By nightfall, we try to sleep, but my sisters and I are so very sad for the teachers and also because we cannot do a thing to help them.

The next morning, my mother prepares our breakfast. I ask Baba to go with me to the village. He agrees, but Mom doesn't want us to go until we have heard word about the teachers. We decide we need to go to the village to find out what is going on. But, once we get there, very few people are out and about their business. They are all holed up in their homes because they are afraid of the Taliban. Baba and I receive no further word about the teachers.

That afternoon, the Taliban return to our village. They bring the kidnapped teachers with them and invite those of us who were out in the village to go to the girls' school. No one wants to go, but they warn us that if we don't get there in five minutes, they will kill us. So, we all go.

Inside the school, the scene is horrific. They behead the teachers in front of everyone. They beheaded two teachers right in front of where I am standing, and I see one teacher's red blood everywhere. I feel sick and faint, and then fall to the ground. My Baba tries to pick me up but the Taliban won't let him. Instead, they drip blood on my face. When I open my eyes again, I see one of the Taliban has a knife and think he is going to behead me. They have finished beheading the seven teachers, and so I cry and beg for them to not behead me too. I cry and cry and cry, unable to control my tears. The Taliban do not allow anyone to help me, and force me to remain on the ground. Through my tears I keep saying, "Don't kill me. I did nothing." In front of me, all I see are the dead teachers. Baba stands by watching this horrible scene, and he is beyond terrified for his son.

Finally, the Taliban believe they have successfully delivered their message to everyone present and allow us to leave. Baba helps me to my feet and we leave in the direction of home. On the way, Baba first takes me to the mosque to get me cleaned up, as I am covered in blood. He washes my face and my clothes the best he can. I am still feeling dizzy and in shock at the horror we had just witnessed. I repeat the same words over and over. "They killed the teachers and they will kill me." My Baba weeps for me and my fear, and for the inexplicable savagery that has occurred.

After I am cleaned up, Baba and I make our way back home. As we approach, Mom comes out to meet us. When sees my face, she knows immediately something is wrong. She, too, cries for me. "What has happened to Hayat?"

Baba cannot bring himself to tell her what happened. But I continue to babble. "They killed the teachers and they will kill me." Baba and Mom manage to get me inside the house. I am still in shock, and unable to sleep or rest in spite of my mother's attempts to calm me down. Every time I close my eyes I see the Taliban and the teacher's blood. In all my fear I am unable to close my eyes. My mother cries for her son and my sisters all cry for their brother.

I ask Baba to have Juma come to our house, telling him I am scared and cannot sleep alone. They all tell me they will sleep with me, but I continue to cry, "I want to see Juma. I want to see Juma." Baba relents and goes to invite Juma to come back to our house. Throughout all this, my head starts to hurt from a terrible headache. After a while, Baba returns home, bringing Juma with him. Juma sees how I am and becomes very sad for me.

Baba decides to take me to the doctor in the Urgun district. Together with Juma, they get me into the car. Juma and I sit in the back seat. I hold my head the entire time. At the doctor's, Baba tells him everything that happened. The doctor is horrified, and cannot believe the Taliban let me live. He then explains to Baba that my head hurts so much because I am so scared. The doctor gives us some drugs and bottles of medicine, including one containing pills to help me sleep. As a normal course of treating patients, doctors always give them medicine to get strong, whether the patient needs it or not. Juma will stay at my home for two or three days, since the school is now closed—thanks to the Taliban.

Baba drives us back home, and I see that my sister Sobia and her husband are there too. Everyone is sad for me. My mom has prepared some food for me, but I am not hungry and do not want to eat a thing. She forces me to eat a bit before taking the medicine the doctor prescribed. When I finish eating, my father gives me the drugs and the medicine to help me sleep. Within five minutes my eyes get heavy and I feel sleepy. I ask Mom to take me and Juma to my room, and we go to sleep. But my sleep is not peaceful. I dream about the Taliban. I watch them behead Juma, and I am crying at the horror. My mom hears my cries from the other room, and she and Baba and my sister come running into my room where they try to wake me from my nightmare. The sleeping medicine is powerful, and I am very groggy and don't know where I am. I continue to cry and scream over and over "They killed Juma."

They all try to calm me and explain that Juma is fine and that he is right here next to me. In my delirium, my heavy eyes remain closed, and I am unable to open them to look around. "They killed Juma. They killed Juma. I saw it with my own eyes. They killed Juma."

Mom gets some water and splashes a bit on my face. I open my eyes and see that Juma is next to me and everyone is crying. I still don't believe that Juma is alive and so I hug him tightly. "They didn't kill you, did they?"

Juma reassures me. "No, Hayat. You were dreaming. I am fine."

I beg my friend to not go anywhere. "Please, Juma, stay with me."

"Yes, I will stay here with you."

It is now midnight, and Mom tells me to go back to sleep. But the visions remain starkly in front of me—the Taliban and the teachers they behead. And so, Juma and I remain awake all night.

The next morning Mom prepares breakfast for everyone. Once again, I am unable to eat. I want nothing more than a glass of water. The mood in my house is very somber as everyone is both sad and worried for me. Baba decides I should go back to the doctor's, and so we return to the Urgun district to see the same doctor we saw the day before. The doctor says it would be better for Baba to take me to the American base because they will have more advanced technology and be better equipped to examine me.

And so we drive to see an American doctor. When Baba arrives at the entry gate, the soldiers take me inside the base and tell Baba and Juma to wait just inside the entrance. I don't understand much of the English they are speaking, and my own English is very limited. The doctor asks me what happened. I attempt to explain, but he doesn't understand my English and asks a translator to help. I tell the translator everything that happened, and he tells the doctor. They give me an injection and then turn on the TV for me. The TV is showing a funny comedy movie, and as I watch it, I forget all the other thoughts that were on my mind. After a while, I feel better, and they allow Baba and Juma to come in to see me. When Baba sees me, he can't believe his eyes. I'm watching this funny movie on TV and laughing!

The doctor has the translator explain to Baba that I should remain at the base for two or three days. Baba agrees to let me stay. But I don't want to stay there alone, so I ask the translator to allow Juma to stay with me. The translator passes my request to the doctor, who accepts. He explains to Baba that he can now leave, and if he wants to visit me, he can come every morning from 9 to 10:30 a.m. And so, Baba leaves, trusting we are in good hands.

Juma and I are now together at the American base. We continue to watch the movie I had been watching earlier. Even though we don't understand what the actors are saying, we laugh because what they are doing is funny. I realize that, after all this time, I am hungry. I really want to eat something, so Juma goes and tells the nurse. The nurse comes to my room and I ask her to bring us some food. She says she will first check with the doctor. In truth, I was not too sick to eat this whole time, just too scared. I had a lot of pressing things on my mind.

The doctor comes to my room and tells me I can eat anything I want. The nurse brings chicken and vegetables. The doctor, who treats me so nicely and kindly, stays and eats with Juma and me. He tells us we can go out and play with the soldiers in the camp when we are done eating. We are happy in the camp, and I never feel that I am not at home. Right now, camp is better for us than home. After a while, the doctor tells the nurse to take us inside the hall to play with the soldiers there. Inside, the soldiers take pictures with Juma and me, and some of them show us photos of their own children. Juma and I have lots of fun at the base. We feel very comfortable there.

We play in the camp until evening when the nurse takes us back to the hospital room. We really enjoy watching TV and ask the nurse to turn it on. She looks for a DVD of a kids' movie, but does not find one in our room. She goes out to look for one, and brings one back that is funnier than the first one we had watched. They soon bring us dinner, and the nurse says that we are to go to sleep when we have finished eating. I tell her "okay" in English, and Juma cannot believe his ears. He says, "Hayat, you should not quit your English class."

After dinner, they give me another shot, and the nurse goes to get some other medicine. When she returns, Juma and I are on the bed watching TV. I feel a bit dizzy and also sleepy, as I had not slept at all the day before. Even though Juma and I are having fun watching the movie together, we both drift off to sleep.

As I awake the next morning, I think I am home and waiting for my mom to wake me. When I open my eyes and am fully awake, I remember I am at the American base camp. I wake Juma. We wash our faces and wait. The nurse arrives at nine o'clock with our breakfast. After breakfast, the doctor comes to check on me.

"How are you feeling today, Hayat?" asked the doctor.

"I feel fine, doctor," I replied in English.

The doctor appears satisfied, but tells me I am to stay there one more day. I am happy to be there, but I also miss my mom. This morning, however, Baba comes to the base, and when he sees me, he is overjoyed because I am now back to my usual self—completely good. Baba stays until 10:30 and then goes back home. He assures me he will tell Mom that I am doing really well. "Hayat and Juma, tomorrow I will come earlier because the doctor will release you to return home."

After Baba leaves, Juma and I go out and play with the soldiers. They seem happy to play with us too. The day goes by quickly, and in the evening, we go back to our hospital room where we repeat everything we had done the night before—the nurse brings us dinner, she turns on the TV, we watch a movie, I have my drugs, and Juma and I both go to sleep.

The next morning, Juma and I wake up early and wait for Baba to arrive. He gets to the base at eight o'clock. Juma and I go to say goodbye to the doctor on our way out. He is a very good man. He tells the nurse to give us toys, and then we walk out the gate where my Baba is waiting.

Back at home, when Mom and my sisters see me, they can't believe the change. They are so happy to have me back to my usual self, and very thankful to the U.S. Army. Juma wants to go home, but I ask him to stay one more day, and the next day we will go to his house.

We go to my room to play with the new toys. I actually have lots of toys I have been given from the American soldiers. Juma, Sadiqullah, and I have fun playing with everything, and Juma and I laugh a lot because Sadiqullah is funny. After playing a long while, my mom brings us lunch. I missed my mother's cooking, especially lunch. Her food is delicious. After lunch Juma and I decide to go out to the farm. While we are out there, Juma asks how long I think our school will be closed. We really don't know, and we are both so sad that we no longer have our school.

After Mosque, my Baba returns home and we all eat dinner together. I tell everyone that I don't miss the hospital dinner, but I sure miss the TV! At that we all laugh. Then I get serious and say, "Baba, you need to do something about the boys' school. Can't you go to the police station in Sarobi and tell them what happened?"

"Hayat and Juma," says Baba, "My cousin works at the police station and they know what happened in our village, but they do nothing about it. We have no one to save us from the Taliban."

"Why won't the Taliban allow us to get educated?" I ask.

"They don't want people to know their real face. If people get educated, then nobody will trust them."

"But, Baba, we already don't trust them."

"Yes, Hayat, this is true," Baba says. "But there are still some people who do."

"What is the religion of the Taliban?" I ask.

"I have no idea. Considering the horrible things the Taliban are doing, I would say they have no religion."

Chapter Eight
2007

Both the boys' and the girls' schools in our village remain closed. Baba needs to go to Urgun District on some business, and I go along with him. We see, for the very first time, that the government is building a wireless telecom network in the Urgun District that will extend and cover much of area of Paktika province. The tower is supposed to be 110–150 meters tall—enormous! We are told the tower will be ready in one month. This means people will be able to use cell phones. I ask Baba what a cell phone is, because I have never seen one. He tells me that once the network is up, we will be able to call home direct from Dubai and, when he is in Dubai, we will be able to call him from home. Once the network is working, we won't need to make or send cassette recordings anymore. I am both amazed and happy when I hear this news.

Baba and I do our shopping. He bought me many things, and when we are finished, we go back home. I tell my sisters and Mom about the cell phones and that in another month we will be able to talk to each other, but they don't believe me. Then Baba explains how the telecom network will work and they are also very happy to hear this good news.

In less than one month, the Afghan wireless cellphone network opens. Baba and I return to the Urgun District to buy cell phones. On our way there, we drive past the new cell tower. "Baba, look how tall the network tower is!"

In 2007, the only cell phone available in our province was the Nokia 1112. We buy two pieces for 11,000 rupees, which was very expensive. Even so, I'm happy! We then buy the SIM cards for each phone. All of this is new to me. I have never seen this technology before. Looking back, I see how special and important the SIM card is. When cell phones first became available in Afghanistan, they were possessions to be kept close, because their limited supply and high cost made buying a replacement difficult. In contrast, today I have three phones and don't worry if I lose one because they are so easily replaced. My Baba is familiar with how all this works from working in Dubai, so he understands how to use the phones and the two SIM cards. He tells me, "Hayat, I heard in Dubai that

Americans have had cell phones for more than fifteen years already. We have one network tower, but they have thousands of them."

Once we have purchased everything we need to use our cell phones, we are ready to go home. Back at home, we put the SIM cards in the phones. Baba tells me to go outside so he can call me to see how the phones work. I run all the way out to our farm. After a minute, I hear the phone ring! I press the green OK button and can hear my Baba talking to me. I just can't believe it! To have these phones and be able to call each other so easily is like a dream for me. I run back home and Baba teaches me about all the buttons and functions on the mobile phone. He also teaches me *Snake*, a special game that comes on Nokia phones. I think I'm in another world. I just can't believe it all.

I am so excited by all this that I decide I need to show Juma my phone. "Baba, I'm going to Juma's to show him my mobile!"

At Juma's I show him my cell phone. It turns out he also got the same one.

"I wanted to go to your house, Hayat, to show you my mobile, but you came here first. Now we both have mobiles and I just can't believe it!" Juma and I discuss the possibilities of calling each other when we want to get together.

Time does not wait. It is February and the Taliban come to our village and make an announcement from the mosque. They tell all the villagers that we are to give them our mobile phones. We are to give our mobile phones to the Taliban, and if we do not, the Taliban will burn down the home of anyone who does not obey.

The Taliban does not want any villager to live in, or exercise, any kind of freedom. Baba gets his mobile for the Taliban, but tells me to hide mine. We give our phone to the Taliban and they write down my father's name on a list as one who gave them his mobile.

Many people from my village bring the mobile phones they have purchased, but many others are poor and cannot afford to buy a mobile phone. The Taliban do not believe these poor people have no phone, and they tell them over and over again to bring their mobiles. These poor villagers try to explain that they don't have any mobile phones, but the Taliban beat them bloody. Now everyone who did not have a mobile to give the Taliban is covered in blood. And then, after everyone who had a mobile phone gives their phone to the Taliban, the Taliban take the phones and crush them all! Yes, once the Taliban has all the phones from the villagers, they break them all. The Taliban are getting stronger, and no one can stand up to them or against them.

When the Taliban leave, the villagers gathered at the masjid beg the imam to do something against the Taliban. "They have broken all our mobile phones and beaten everyone who did not have one to give them. Why did they beat the people who do not have mobile phones?"

I thought at first that the Taliban were taking our mobiles to use for themselves, which might have been understandable. But instead they just smash them into the ground? I don't understand what is happening. Smashing the mobiles is senseless. Why don't they use them? Nothing in my country makes sense any more.

Our imam is sad for the people who lost their phones and for those who were beaten, but even our beloved imam cannot change the Taliban or fix their levels of cruelty toward the villagers.

We walk home, but are sad and despondent because of the Taliban. They just don't want us civilians to live our own lives. Back at home, Mom gets us dinner and then I go to bed.

In the morning, I see American soldiers are talking with our imam. A crowd of men has gathered nearby. Our imam tells the translator to explain to the U.S. Army that the Taliban come to our village to threaten and terrorize the people every day. They closed the girls' school. They closed the boys' school. They killed seven teachers. They took everyone's cell phones and smashed them on the ground. They beat the people who said they did not own cell phones.

The soldiers tell us that the villagers must all stand with them against the Taliban. The imam agrees. He asks those gathered, "Who wants to stand against the Taliban?" Many of the young men present—at least forty-six of them—are ready to work with the U.S. Army to stand and fight against the Taliban.

The next step is for the U.S. Army to conduct eye exams of every man who has volunteered to fight. These men then all go with the U.S. soldiers to their base to get registration cards and weapons to fight the Taliban. They will remain on the base over night to learn how to use the weapons. The mood of the people in the village is lighter now that we are going to stand against the Taliban.

At ten o'clock the next morning, the men who went with the U.S. Army to get their weapons return to the village. Our own villagers are now prepared to defend our village, and the Army returns to the Urgun base.

Two months pass with no visit from the Taliban, so the imam decides to open the boys' school again. That is not to say we no longer fear the Taliban, because many do. But my Baba tells me I am to go to school the next day. I'm scared to go. The Taliban are such animals they don't know about humanity or have any respect for human life.

"Baba, can I first see if Juma is going, and if he is, then I will go too?" Baba agrees. I go to see Juma and tell him that we should go to school in the morning. Juma is really afraid and refuses to go. But I am stubborn and force the argument on him to go with me. He eventually agrees to go. I tell Juma to get his school bag and come stay at my house that night, and then we will go to school together in the morning.

The next day Juma and I are up early and leave for school after breakfast. We have a lot of fear in our hearts as we approach our school. Only the two teachers from the old school remain and many students did not come. In fact, only a few students are present. The teacher tells us we will all move to the next grade level without taking our final exams from the previous school year. Upon hearing this, everyone is happy because that means we don't have to take our final exams.

School continues like this with two teachers and thirty-eight students. Every villager has bought another cell phone, and we all have the phone numbers of the village soldiers, so if anyone hears any information about the Taliban, they can call and inform the village soldiers or the imam. People seem to be happier now and most students have decided to return to school. Only a few students have made the decision to remain at home, and the girls' school remains completely closed.

For three months, everything is fine and we go to school every day. One night, Juma comes over after school and spends the night. At midnight, we are awakened to the sound of weapons in the village. My whole family is now awake and we call the village soldiers. Nobody answers the phone because they are fighting the Taliban. Three hundred Taliban are fighting against a mere forty-seven village soldiers. The imam is on the loudspeaker asking people to help the village soldiers because there are too many Taliban and many of the village soldiers are dead.

When my father hears this, he grabs his AK47 to go help. My mom tries to stop him but he doesn't listen. He goes out to the village, but we have no idea the direction from which the Taliban are shooting. We know they have big weapons. They are targeting homes, people, everything in the village, but still my Baba goes outside. We are all screaming and crying. We have no idea who is killed and who isn't. Three hours later, the imam again calls from the loudspeaker for help because of the high numbers of Taliban fighters.

Soon we hear the sound of U.S. Army fighter jets. We have no idea who informed them, but they are bombing the mountains. The attacks from the Taliban slow down somewhat, but continue nevertheless. It is now sunrise and the Taliban have retreated. Juma and I run to the village, and I see my Baba is also there. I run to him, thankful he is still alive. The villagers now come out to see who has been killed. Nine of the village soldiers are dead and four more are badly injured. Up to thirty-four of the Taliban are dead. Baba gets our car to transport the wounded village soldiers to the hospital at the base in Urgun. Before he leaves, a woman runs out of the imam's house and tells the men gathered that three women inside are injured. We are now all worried that the Taliban were targeting the imam's family.

At noon, we are all waiting to hear from the government, but we see the U.S. Army is on their way to us. They go to the imam's house and see many rooms have been destroyed. They give the imam some cash so he can rebuild his home.

The Army tells us not to give up. Our people are now angry at the Taliban and say they will never give up. The American soldiers give the village soldiers new weapons for fighting the Taliban. Now every home has two or three young men who stand with the village soldiers to fight and protect their families and our village.

Some of the villagers take our dead soldiers away to be buried. Juma and I go back to my home. The fear of the Taliban we had in our hearts is now gone. Back home, my mom tells Juma and me a story. This is the second time our villagers have fought against the Taliban. The first war between the Taliban and our village was when the Russians left Afghanistan in 1989. The Taliban arrived in Afghanistan and were fighting against the Hazbi Islami, who wanted to combat communism in Afghanistan. The Taliban won the war against them. The Russians had a camp in our mountains which was called Taboot Kararga, and that base was taken by our village. The Taliban wanted a third base, but our villagers wouldn't move. The Taliban fought our villagers who, at that time, were strong because they had possession of all the weapons left behind at the base by the Russians.

Mom told me I was three years old at the time. On the first day of fighting, our villagers killed a lot of the Taliban, even though there were only four hundred of us against two thousand Taliban. On the second day, the Taliban were much stronger and they succeeded at capturing the base. But that night, we took it back. This fight went on for three days. In the end, our villagers had to leave everything behind and flee to the village of Rabat for safety. My Baba was in Dubai, but my paternal grandfather was alive, so he was the one who took care of our home. He left us safely in Rabat and came back to our village to fight the Taliban, who were very strong at the time. They killed sixty-seven people from our village, one of whom was my grandpa. They killed Grandpa with a rocket. Our people took just half of his body to the grave to be buried because that is all that was left. Grandpa and the other village fighters put their weapons down to the Taliban, which meant we lost the war because the Taliban was stronger. They were supported by Pakistan and able to take the Taboot Kararga base from our villagers.

After two months, our villagers called a town meeting to tell the Taliban to allow the people of the village to return to their homes. On the first request, the Taliban would not allow it, but they finally did. This is the short story of my grandpa.

So now my Baba comes home and announces he has decided to stand against the Taliban with the village soldiers. We now have some five hundred village soldiers. We get to go to school every day and the imam eventually decides to bring in new teachers—for the girls' school as well as for ours. They open the girls' school again because we now have a large group of village soldiers and they protect the village from the Taliban.

Chapter Nine
2008

Juma and I are now studying in grade level 8. We are not receiving any threats from the Taliban, and we are living in peace. In addition, Juma and I are growing up. For the first time, my Baba teaches me how to drive. Driving is not easy. In fact, I find it just as hard as the first time I learned to ride my bicycle. At first, I am just unable to master driving. But after three days, I finally learn how to properly manage the clutch and the brakes and change gears to drive. And so now I am a driver—just like that. In Afghanistan, we don't get a driver's license. My father doesn't have one. Come to think of it, I don't know anyone who has one. And of course, women do not drive. They don't drive and they don't leave their house.

I am happy now that I am able to drive. I can go to the market to shop for my family and I can pick up Juma. We often go to the Urgun district together, as we are doing that day. I buy everything my mother tells me to.

Back at home my mom is very happy. "You are now becoming a man, Hayat," she tells me.

"No, I'm still young, Mom."

She laughs at that, and brings us our lunch. Juma and I eat and talk about our upcoming exams. After lunch, we study for a bit. When Juma says it's time for him to go home, I tell him I will drive him. It only takes five minutes to get to his house by car!

Exam day arrives, and I find the exam to be very hard. Juma and I both finish and start another three-month vacation. After lunch, I go to the village where I remain until evening when I go to the mosque for prayer. After prayer, I head back home. The weather is cold now, so I go to sleep right after dinner to warm up under my covers. Before falling asleep, I think about our village and how safe it is. It has been this way for some time. Finally.

Chapter Ten
2009

Juma and I are once again headed to school, happy to be starting grade level 9. My sisters are also on their way to school. I am also happy to find out that we have English class on the very first day of school.

After school, I return home for lunch and then drive to pick up Juma to go to the Sarobi District, where we hang out with friends and try to act cool.

The next day we have school again, but it is also the day everyone registers their voting card for the upcoming election. My family and I also register our voting card, which is for men only. Later that evening, Baba feels ill and decides to stay home rather than go help the village soldiers. By ten o'clock we have finished dinner and I go to bed.

No one is able to sleep because the Taliban have once again started to fight with our villagers. They are very close and the sounds of shots being fired gets to be too much. Baba gets his AK-47 to go out to the village and help fight against the Taliban. Mom begs him not to go and tries to prevent him from leaving. But Baba pays no attention to her pleading.

Mom cries, "If you go outside, I will kill myself!"

Baba looks at her and yells back in anger, "Go ahead and kill yourself! It is my duty to help save our village!" Before that moment, I had never heard my father yell at my mother. In our village, men never yell at women.

As he prepares to leave, I tell him I want to go with him, but he stops me. The fighting is very close to our home and we hear the firing of the guns as if it were right outside our door. I don't listen to Baba, even though he keeps telling me to stay at home. My mother and sisters are all scared and crying, and even my little brother Sadiqullah is now awake and crying. Everyone tries to stop Baba and me, but we are both determined to go out and fight.

Mom pleads again, "Please, don't go out there. What about your son Sadiqullah? He needs his father."

Baba says nothing. He does not even look at her. The firing is now right outside the main gate to our home, approximately twenty feet away. Baba loads the AK-47, hands me a flashlight, and tells me to go up to the roof. I climb the stairs to the roof with Baba following right behind. From our rooftop, Baba fires his gun toward the main gate of our house. We immediately hear men's voices below.

"We are not Taliban! Stop shooting!"

I yell to Baba, "They are village soldiers, Baba! Stop firing!"

Baba is not deterred because he knows how the Taliban cheat and lie. "Hayat, they are just saying this to get me to stop shooting at them. They are Taliban!"

I am appalled to hear this and tell Baba, "I will jump over to the next roof to see if I can tell who they are." I move to the next roof and shine my flashlight down on the men at our gate. I see they are villagers and yell back to Baba, "They are village soldiers! Don't shoot anymore!"

Baba is still very serious, but now a bit calmer. "Go down and open the door for them, Hayat."

I do as I am told. The next thing we know, thirteen village soldiers are standing inside our house. They talk briefly and decide they will be able to fight more easily from our rooftop. Everyone, including Baba and me, head back up to the roof. We have no idea which side the Taliban are coming from, and Baba says we shouldn't shoot until we know what direction they're coming from. Everyone agrees and stops firing.

"I have the phone number for the Urgun base. I can call them for help," I say.

"Yes, Hayat. Call them now," says Baba.

I go back downstairs to make the call. When I dial the number on my mobile phone, I realize the network is not working. "I cannot believe the network is down—right now, when we need it the most!" I remove the SIM card, wait a few seconds, and put it back in, thinking that might help, but nothing. The network is simply not working at this time.

I return to the roof and tell my father that I was unable to make the call because the mobile network is not working. By now the Taliban are getting closer to our village and we don't know what to do. Then Baba has an idea. He takes one of the flares and fires it toward the Urgun base, hoping this serves as a message to the U.S. Army that there is fighting in our village. He also fires thirty bullets from a gun in the direction of the Urgun base, but even with all that, we still receive no response from the Americans. By now it is midnight. Baba and the other soldiers decide to go out to the village.

"Hayat, you must stay home now. I am not alone, so I will be fine." My little brothers are frightened from all the sounds of guns firing, and everyone is upset and crying. Mom and I together try to comfort them but it is impossible. We continue like this until three in the morning, with the shooting and fighting going on outside, and the tears and worrying going on inside.

We finally hear the sound of helicopters and I look outside to see what they do. We later learn the U.S. Army was sending two helicopters from their base in the village of Shkin to the base in Urgun. The helicopters were not sent to help us. But the Taliban do not know this. They think the helicopters have come to help the villagers and they start shooting at them. The soldiers in the helicopters are taken by surprise and have no idea who is shooting at them, so they return fire. But, because the Americans don't know who is shooting from the ground, they target anyone and everyone. Our village soldiers all run for cover, with many of them pouring into our house.

By now the U.S. soldiers have called their base to tell them about the fighting in our village, and soon two more helicopters arrive. These two fly over our house and see all the men entering our front gate. Our house happens to be located near the mountains where some Taliban are probably hiding. And because the U.S. soldiers saw so many fighters enter our house, they believe these men are Taliban and they are also hiding here. By dawn, all four helicopters are hovering at our house and dropping soldiers to our roof and to the ground. My mother and sisters are so frightened they cannot stop crying. I, too, am scared, but I don't cry.

We hear a voice from outside. A translator is speaking through a loudspeaker from one of the helicopters. He says, "Come outside! Bring your weapons! If not, we will shoot!"

Inside, we all look at each other and know what we must do. The village soldiers all step outside. My entire family, including Mom, my sisters, and my little brothers also go outside. With everyone gathered in our courtyard, the Americans shine a bright light down on us from their helicopter. They can see us but we cannot see them. We realize there are American soldiers on our roof, and we yell over and over that we are not Taliban. "We are village soldiers!"

The Americans tell us to set our weapons down, which we do. They enter our courtyard and tie us all up by our hands. Because I know a little English, I tell them we are all village soldiers. But the Americans still do not trust us. The translator enters the courtyard and now Baba explains our situation to him. Thankfully, Baba has convinced the translator that we are who we say we are. The translator tells the Americans that we really are not Taliban and they immediately free our hands. The translator asks my father why we did not call the base. Baba tells them that we tried to call but the network was down. One of the American soldiers checks our phone and confirms the network is indeed down. The sun is now almost risen, and this is how our day begins.

The U.S. soldiers leave our home and head for the village, where more American soldiers are waiting. The village soldiers also leave our home to do a check around the village. They find nine dead village soldiers and eleven unaccounted for. Five bodies of Taliban shot by our village soldiers are found at the outskirts of the village, and seventeen more bodies of dead Taliban are found near the jungle. These men were killed by the soldiers in the helicopters.

Everyone gathered looks for the missing village soldiers. One of the missing is my Baba's cousin. We spend the entire day searching for them, and still do not find them by the time night starts to fall. The darkness does not stop us. Both the U.S. and village soldiers continue searching all night long, but come up empty handed. The next morning, the village soldiers ask the U.S. Army to go into the mountains with them to look for the missing soldiers. The Americans agree and accompany the village soldiers into the mountains.

The remaining villagers anxiously await their return. At two o'clock, the U.S. and village soldiers return. They bring with them the bodies of our eleven missing soldiers. But the worst part is that the bodies have no heads. The Taliban beheaded these men and kept their heads for themselves. The people in my village are horrified at this and cry out of helplessness and fear.

The imam from our mosque steps forward and tells everyone to stop crying. "We have to make a sacrifice to protect our village. These men sacrificed their lives on our behalf. We will not give up. As soon as we bury our soldiers, we will take revenge on the Taliban for their horrific actions."

An American soldier gives the imam a satellite phone. They explain that this phone will always work, even when our mobile network is down. They assure us they will help us when we call, and then leave to return to their base. The rest of us go home. We have not slept in two days, and Baba and I walk home in silence. Mom tells Baba he should eat something, but Baba tells her he is too tired to eat and wants only to sleep. With that, Baba and I both go to bed where we fall asleep in minutes from sheer exhaustion. We sleep for most of the day.

* * *

That evening, my Baba tells me that I need to go to Dubai.

I am upset to hear him say this. "What about school, Baba? I have not yet finished."

He tells me, "Hayat, in this country, no one can truly learn by going to school."

I look to my mother for support. "Mom, I really don't want to go to Dubai—not yet."

But both Mom and Baba force the issue. It is settled. I will go to Dubai. Next Baba says he will accompany me to Paktika Province so I can get my passport. That I have to leave home and go to Dubai is all because of the Taliban.

"And tomorrow, Hayat, we will go to Urgun to have your passport pictures taken."

The next morning, I am still sad by the news that I must drop out of school to go to work in Dubai. On our drive to Urgun I tell Baba that I want to complete my education here first.

"Don't worry, Hayat. You will still be able to study in Dubai."

That news cheers me up a bit, but I am still sad because I don't want to leave my mom or my family. We arrive in Urgun where I get my passport pictures taken, and then we return home. We will travel to Paktika Province the next day to obtain my passport.

* * *

The next morning, Baba and I make the four-hour drive to Paktika Province. It is a long trip, but we finally arrive at the Ministry of Passports, located in Paktika Province center. The governor does not approve me to get a passport. He says I am too young to leave our country for business, but Baba tells him the entire story of how I witnessed the Taliban beheading people at my school and that I had to be hospitalized as a result of the trauma I suffered from that experience. The governor still refuses, but then says that if Baba pays him twenty thousand rupees, he will change my age on the passport and make me older than I really am.

"No! I will not do that!" says Baba.

"Then leave!" says the governor.

Baba turns to leave but then stops when he realizes we have no choice. He pays the governor the money and the governor marks my age on the passport as twenty-two, even though I am much younger. We hand the governor my photos, and he tells us to return the next day at the same time and my passport will be ready. Baba and I leave the Ministry of Passports and go to the Sharan market. There is a restaurant in this area that also rents out rooms. Baba pays two hundred rupees and we have a room for one night.

In the morning, we return to the Ministry of Passports to pick up my passport. We have to pay another three thousand rupees, the cost for a legal passport—only mine is not so legal. When we finish at the Ministry, we find a phone so my father can call his brother, my Uncle Ibrahim, in Dubai. Baba wants a fax number so we can send him a copy of my new passport. My uncle tells my father he will call us back in five minutes, once he confirms a good fax number we can use. A few minutes later, my uncle calls back and gives Baba the fax number to use. From there, we go to a small market shop that has a fax machine and have a copy of my passport faxed to Uncle Ibrahim.

Our errands in Paktika Province are all done, and Baba and I make the long drive home. On the way, Baba talks to me about Dubai. He tells me Dubai is one of the most beautiful cities in the world. He is trying to cheer me up and get me excited about going. Well, his plan worked, because I am now looking forward to going, thanks to all the beautiful stories Baba told me.

We arrive back home later that day. I show Mom and my sisters my passport. Though they see my age is indicated as twenty-two, they say nothing to Baba about this, as they know it is his decision, and to cross him would be disrespectful. Now all I need is my Dubai travel visa. Later, I tell Juma everything that is happening. He is shocked and sad that I must go to Dubai, as he feels he is losing his best friend.

* * *

Just a few days remain before our presidential elections are to take place. One night, we are all home sleeping, except for Baba, who is out, as usual, with the village soldiers. After breakfast the next morning, I go out to look for Baba in the village. Even though it is still early, I see a lot of people gathered at the mosque. They are talking about a note left there by the Taliban. The note says that whoever casts a vote in the upcoming election will be punished by having their fingers cut off.

The imam tells everyone he believes someone from our village is helping the Taliban. When he says this, we all look around at each other, because we have no idea who it could be or who would want to do something so horrible to his neighbors. On our way home, Baba is worried, of course, but he is thinking hard, trying to come up with the name of the person who could be helping the Taliban.

That night, Baba returns home early from his night out working with the village soldiers. We are all asleep, but he wakes us up to tell us what is going on.

"The U.S. Army has come to the village. They told the village soldiers to all go home and to not go back out until the morning."

We do not know what is going on, but we do as we are told. The next morning, we hear news that the people who were helping the Taliban have been caught. The American soldiers tell us that people from three homes in our village were helping the Taliban—men named Zafer, Ghulam, and Naiz. But these men were doing much more than just helping the Taliban. They were, in fact, fighting for them.

The imam tells us to go ask the families of these men if they are also involved with the Taliban, and if they are, they must leave our village. Everyone agrees with what the imam tells us to do. We go to each of the three homes and ask the families if they are involved. Everyone swears to God that they knew nothing about their family members helping the Taliban. The people report back to the imam that the families say they have nothing to do with the Taliban and they had no idea about their family member's involvement. The imam directs the village soldiers to always remain alert and to keep their eyes on these three homes.

* * *

Election day is here. Because we were threatened by the Taliban, village soldiers are everywhere, out en masse to protect voters from this evil. Members of the U.S. Army and the Afghan police also come to our village that day. As they were traveling to our village, a bomb placed by the Taliban exploded, killing two Afghan policemen and three U.S. soldiers, and wounding four others. We were saddened to hear this had happened, but heartened to know these forces still come to our village to help protect us so we can vote. People vote—many for Hamid Karzai—in spite of the Taliban threat that they will cut off people's fingers.

Voting continues until two p.m. when the voting station closes down. At that time, the U.S. soldiers and the Afghan police leave the village, and Baba and I walk back home. Along the way, I ask Baba to call my uncle to check on the status of my visa. At home Baba calls my uncle who tells him that my visa application was denied—twice.

"Hayat, your uncle is trying a third time. He told me he is sure this time your visa will be approved."

It is August, and I wait quietly and patiently, not really certain I want the visa approved. My enthusiasm from the day Baba told me all those wonderful stories about Dubai has waned. In a matter of days, I am in the village when my uncle calls Baba and tells him my visa has been issued. When I return home, Baba tells me what he thinks is good news.

"You will be leaving for Dubai in a few days, Hayat, traveling there with a villager who is here from Dubai on vacation. His name is Fazal Khan."

I am not as excited to go to Dubai as I was at first. That night, I lie awake thinking about Juma and how alone he will be if I go to Dubai.

In the morning, I plan to go see Fazal Khan to ask him when we will leave for Dubai. On the way, I pick up Juma and tell him about my visa. Juma gets very sad, and tells me not to leave during Ramadan. It is my turn to get sad when I explain that my visa has been issued and I must go to Dubai before it expires.

At Fazal Khan's house, he tells me we will be leaving in two days. Juma and I drive home in silence. My thoughts go back to the day we found the nest in the jungle and took the baby birds to care for them. Then I think about our burfis—the letters we race to deliver at the first snow of the season—and wonder if I will ever do another one with my family again. These are such simple moments, but the memories of these times with my family and with Juma are as fresh as if the events happened yesterday.

Back at home I ask permission to go to the Urgun market to buy some new clothes for Dubai. Baba lets me go, and Juma and I go shopping. Afterwards, we return to my house and I ask Juma to stay with me for my last two days in the village.

The next morning, Baba goes to the market in Sarobi to buy a goat to sacrifice on my behalf before I leave home. Juma and I go to my sister Sobia's house to invite her to the sacrifice that will take place the next day. She had not heard the news that I was going to Dubai. I tell Sobia the entire story of everything that has happened, and she is very sad for me. She brings us tea, after which she accompanies us back home.

By the time we arrive, Baba has already returned. He has been telling everyone about Dubai and that I will be leaving in another day. I am so upset about being forced to leave, I don't want to listen to anything my Baba says. The plan is to sacrifice the goat in the morning, but we must ask for help from our neighbors.

* * *

The next morning, Juma and I have breakfast and then go to our neighbor's house to ask for help in sacrificing the goat. Once that task has been completed, my mother cooks the goat with rice. We invite some people from the village, including my teachers and the imam, to join us at that night's meal. Once everyone is gathered in our home, several of our guests—specifically, my teachers—tell Baba not to let my talent go to waste.

"Hayat should continue his studies."

"Hayat has a good future here in Afghanistan."

Baba dismisses those objections by reminding everyone of the constant civil war we are under. "And besides, once he is in Dubai, he will continue with his studies."

My teachers are happy to hear this and I am relieved. I don't want all my studies to go to waste either. I have come so far with my school work, and I want to continue on as long as I can.

After dinner, everyone wishes me a safe journey, and then they leave—except for Juma.

Baba says, "Hayat and Juma, tomorrow we will all go together as far as the capital of Kabul, but then we must leave Hayat to continue his journey on his own. From there he will fly to Dubai accompanied by Fazal Khan."

* * *

In the morning, even before breakfast, my mom tells me I should go visit my grandfather's grave, since he loved me more than anyone else. Juma and I go to the grave together, and I spend several minutes praying to my grandfather.

Back at home, Mom has breakfast all prepared for Juma and me, and we sit down to eat. I look around at my mother and sisters, and say, "I don't want any of you to cry. If you do, I will not go to Dubai." I can tell they are about to cry, but thankfully they are able to control themselves and hold back their tears.

At eight o'clock, Baba goes out to start the car. Fazal Khan has arrived and is waiting outside. Inside, I say my goodbyes to my family. I will never forget this moment, as it was sad for us all and everyone is crying. My mom tries not to cry in front of me so as not to upset me. But when I step outside, I feel my mother breaking down from the heavy sadness she is feeling.

After driving all day, we finally reach Kabul. The city has completely changed from when I was last there in 2003. What strikes me most is that women are out on the streets shopping, something that never happens in my village. But, of course! The Taliban are not present in Kabul to stop them.

We find a hotel and make a reservation for the night. We then go out and find a travel agency to buy our airplane tickets. We buy tickets from Ariana Afghan Airline because they are the best, most reliable airline in Afghanistan. We then have dinner at the hotel and go to our room for the night. Baba says I need to get a good night's sleep in preparation for my trip in the morning.

"We will leave here by 8:30," says Baba, "because we must be at the airport by 9:00 a.m. Your flight leaves at 12:30." I already miss my mother because she always wakes me up in the morning.

* * *

Everything is on schedule in the morning, and by 8:30 we are in the car heading to the airport. I realize I have just thirty minutes left with my Baba and my best friend. We reach the entrance gate, and Baba and Juma are not allowed to go beyond that point. We take turns saying goodbye, and Juma and I are both crying. Our sadness at this moment is overwhelming. Baba looks at the two of us, best friends for so many years, and I think his heart breaks for us because he, too, cries. Fazal Khan is the only one who is not crying, and he tells us we must finish our goodbyes, as it is time to go. He and I walk through the gate, but I am unable to control myself. I take just a few steps before turning around and running back to Juma to give him one final hug.

"Hayat," says Baba, "you must go now."

I give Baba one final hug and turn and walk away with Fazal Khan. Baba and Juma head toward the exit door. The next time I turn around, they are no longer in sight. That moment was the saddest I had ever felt. My life—and how I lived with Juma and Baba—has ended.

*   *   *

I stay close by Fazal as we continue on through the airport. We head to the check-in counter where our bags are checked. From there, we go through immigration control without any problem and take a seat in the waiting area. I check the time and see it is already noon. The next thing I know, we hear an announcement for everyone who is waiting to board the plane to get on a bus. I follow Fazal without question. The bus takes us to the airplane that is farthest out on the tarmac. A flight attendant shows us to our seats. I am in seat F13.

As this is my first time on an airplane, I have no idea what is happening or what to do. I remind myself that Baba does this all the time. Fazal tells me not to worry about a thing.

"I am fine," I tell him, although actually I am quite frightened. The attendants tell everyone to tighten their seat belts, but I don't know how to do it, so an attendant helps me. I then close my eyes as I wait for takeoff. The airplane engine starts and I feel us starting to move very slowly. Soon the airplane picks up speed and takes off. I open my eyes, but my head spins as the airplane turns in the air, so I close them again. After a few minutes, I open my eyes again and see that the airplane is now straight. An attendant announces that we will arrive in Dubai in two and a half hours.

After one hour in the air, the hosts serve everyone food. I am hungry and eat everything on the tray, after which I fall asleep. I sleep until it is almost time to land, as one of the flight attendants wakes me up and tells me to tighten my seat belt again. This time I remember how to do it. Before long, the plane lands. I'm scared during the landing, but soon the pilot brakes and everything comes to a stop. My first flight is over.

As soon as the plane comes to a stop, everyone unbuckles their seat belt and stands to get their bags. Fazal Khan and I do the same. As at the airport in Kabul, we get off the plane and onto a bus that takes us to the airport. But the heat outside is tremendous and I feel as though I am on fire. I can hardly breathe it is so hot! Dubai is a large, modern city, and is mostly concrete and asphalt, so the temperatures are extreme. The average temperature in Dubai in summer is 113° Fahrenheit (45° Centigrade). And, because of Dubai's proximity to the sea, humidity levels average eighty-five to ninety percent. The temperatures in Afghanistan are similar, but the humidity levels are much lower.

I remember that Baba had given me a SIM card for Dubai, so I put it in my cell phone. Inside immigration, Fazal tells me to show the agent a copy of my visa and they will let me keep the original, which I do. The agent then tells me to go to the next counter for an eye exam. They test my eyes and apparently, my vision is fine. From there I am told to go straight to the final counter to have my passport stamped.

The man at that counter looks first at me, then at photo in the passport and the age noted in the passport. He says something to me in Arabic, which I don't understand. He then speaks to me in English. "Why do you look so different from the age indicated in your passport?"

I comprehend what he has asked me in English, but pretend to not understand English either, so the agent eventually just stamps my passport and lets me through customs. I was distracted by all this, and now look for Fazal Kahn, but I have lost sight of him. I have no idea where to go. I approach an airport security guard and ask him in Pashto where the exit is. The guard walks with me and tells me to look toward the left, where I see a sign that indicates the exit. I then remember to check my phone. I see that Baba has called me twenty-three times! I never even heard the phone ring once! The phone has been silent this entire time. But now I call my Uncle Ibrahim, who is meeting me at the airport. My uncle is upset with me, wondering where I am. I tell him I am on my way out of the airport.

"Hayat, go straight out the door and then turn right," he tells me.

I do as my uncle says and see him waiting for me along with Fazal Khan! I am so relieved to see him. He gives me a big hug and is happy to see me, but at the same time he scolds me for not answering my phone. We get in a taxi and head to what will be my new home. Dubai is beautiful, just like my Baba said. I look at everything as we drive home from the airport, hardly paying any attention at all to what my uncle is saying—just like at home, when I don't listen to what anyone is saying at lunchtime because I am always too busy eating.

I am absolutely amazed to see that women drive! I have never seen that before. I keep looking at everything all around me, but I also see the streets are packed with traffic. I see tall, tall buildings, and feel as though

I am dreaming. I can't believe this is real life. After driving for twenty-five minutes, we reach Deira, Dubai, which is the part of the city where my uncle lives. He takes my bag and, together with Fazal Khan, we enter his home. New things for me are beds for sleeping and a stove for cooking. At home in Afghanistan, I only sleep on the floor and my mom and sisters cook all our meals from holes in the ground with an open fire.

One of my mother's cousins also lives with my uncle. His name is Wali Jan, and he is also happy to see me. Of course, there are no women in the house, as they must all remain in the home country. Wali Jan goes to a restaurant to pick up lunch and bring it back to the house for us. I'm glad to hear that because I am very hungry. By now it is 3:30 in the afternoon and Fazal Khan is ready to return to his own home. My uncle invites him to stay and have lunch with us, and Fazal Khan agrees. After lunch, Fazal Khan leaves and my uncle tells me I should rest. I am feeling tired and am certain I could easily fall asleep. My uncle shows me the bed where I am to sleep. Because I have slept only on the floor my entire life, I don't know how to sleep on a bed. The one exception was when I was in the hospital. I was in a bed there, and Juma stayed in it with me. I try to sleep in the bed at my uncle's house, but I am just not able to fall asleep. In fact, I fall out of the bed! Every time I try to sleep on a bed, I fall out of it—to this very day.

At six o'clock that same evening, my uncle tells me to take a shower and get cleaned up because he wants to take me out to see more of Dubai. I go to the washroom, but I find that the water in the shower is much too hot. Everything in Dubai is hot, and I am simply unable to shower because the hot water will make me feel even hotter! I decide to just change my clothes instead, and tell my uncle I am ready to go out into the big city.

The first place my uncle takes me is to our shop, which is a ten-minute walk from home along Al Nakheel Street. Dubai was built on the trading mentality and economy, and is the center of textile trading in the Middle East. In our shop, we are fabric traders and sell fabrics from all over the world. The shop measures ten feet by twenty feet, and is one of hundreds of others just like it. The shop has one salesman, Obaid Khan, and my uncle introduces us. I notice that it is very hot inside the shop.

"Uncle, why is it so hot in our shop?"

"We don't have AC, Hayat."

"What is AC, Uncle?"

At that, my uncle laughs. "It is a machine that cools the air."

I don't remember hearing or learning about air conditioning in my village at home. "How can you make the air conditioning work? The temperature here is at least up to 48 degrees." The idea of a machine that can blow cold air inside a room or a house when the outside temperature is so hot is hard for me to comprehend.

My uncle explains that our shop is not the only one without any air conditioning. None of the shops in the market have air conditioning. I am amazed to think that not one of the 263 shops in the market has air conditioning. My uncle also tells me that this market was once located in Sabakha, closer to his home, but a fire occurred in April 2008 that gutted 183 shops. In July 2008, they moved the market to this location just five hundred meters away, while the government of Dubai works on building a new permanent market.

"It was better than being jobless, Hayat. So, we work here, even if it means we must withstand all the heat."

I am happy to hear the government is building a new market, but disappointed to learn that it won't be ready till the following year. My uncle and I walk through the market and I cheer up when I realize that many people from my village work here.

"Uncle, can you take me to Juma's brother's shop?" He agrees, and we go see Eid, who is really happy to see me and happy that I'm in Dubai. He gets my uncle and me each a cool drink and then asks me about his family back at home in the village, especially Juma. I tell him that everyone from his home is fine, even Juma. "Yes, Juma and my Baba remained with me on my journey up to Kabul." Eid is so happy to hear the good news about his family.

At home in my village, I was used to eating dinner early and then going straight to bed. In Dubai, my stomach is still on that same clock, and I tell my uncle I am hungry, as it is nighttime. He takes me to a restaurant for breakfast, and explains that I have to eat breakfast now because dinner time in Dubai is at midnight. Even the shops don't close until 11:30 at night! All this activity occurs so late at night because it is too hot to be out during the day. This is all very different for me.

After I finish my breakfast, my uncle tells me we will go home and that his salesman will close up shop for the day. It is still very hot outside, and back at home my uncle tells me to take another shower. I say nothing about the water being too hot, and instead of taking a shower, I wash only my hands and face.

The cook at my uncle's house is from India, and he cooks us a delicious dinner. By one a.m. I am tired and ready for bed. I remember I'm supposed to sleep in a bed, and feel that I just won't be able to fall asleep. But, I have no choice. I get into bed and eventually fall asleep. After a while, I fall out of bed and wake everyone in the household with my screams. "I just cannot sleep here. I want to go home!" I shout. But my uncle calms me and I finally fall back to sleep.

I must have been tired because I sleep until eleven in the morning when my uncle wakes me to tell me he is going to the shop. "I want to go with you," I tell him.

"No, Hayat. Not for a few days. Right now, you go with Wali Jan to the park." Uncle Ibrahim gives me some money, and Wali Jan and I go to Al Mamzar Beach Park. We take a twenty-minute taxi ride to the park, which turns out to be another amazing discovery for me. This park is enormous and, what's more, it is also a beach. This is the first time I have ever seen a beach. At home, we are surrounded only by mountains. So here, for the first time ever, I see sandy beaches and wave after wave of water hitting the beach. I also see, for the first time, both men and women swimming at the beach. I am struck by the differences between women here and women and girls at home—to see women wearing bathing suits and exposing their bodies is truly shocking to me.

"Wali Jan, with everything I see in Dubai, how is it that the Taliban won't even let girls go to school? I see girls swimming at the beach and I also see they drive."

"Hayat, actually, Dubai is very different from our country and village. There are many more differences that you will see in time."

Wali Jan and I go swimming and I find the water to be very salty. But I love it and am happy at the beach. We stay there all afternoon and return home in the evening. On the ride home, I play over and over in my mind the fact that I was actually swimming at a beach. I still cannot believe it!

After being home a while, I get bored and ask Wali Jan to take me to my uncle's shop. He agrees, and we are there in ten minutes.

The streets here are all very busy with so much going on. Everything is very busy and very noisy. When my uncle sees me, he asks, "Hayat, what are you doing? Why did you come here now?"

I tell him I was bored at home and that I wanted to take a walk to see everything that is so interesting along the streets. I remain at the shop with the Obaid the salesman for the remainder of the evening.

* * *

August 21, 2009 – Ramadan is about to start. Once we conclude the Isha prayer this evening, that is, the last of the five prayers that comprise the daily prayer ritual of all practicing Muslims, the holy month of Ramadan will begin. During Ramadan, we fast—no food or drink—from sunrise to sunset, pray, and spend time on introspection during which we avoid impure thoughts and any type of behavior that negates the reward we receive by fasting. In the pre-dawn hours and in the evening, we break our day-long fast by sharing a meal with our family and friends.

The warm temperature and lack of air conditioning in our shop makes fasting difficult. The temperature ranges between 45 and 48 degrees Celsius, which is 113 to 118 degrees Fahrenheit, but we have to continue our fast. We go to the mosque and then return to the shop after prayer. Our shop closing and opening times have changed, and now all the shops remain open until one o'clock in the morning. After we close the shop, we have breakfast and get our eating in before sunrise to keep our Ramadan fast going.

Back at home, my uncle and Wali Jan both tell me I should not fast. They believe I am too young and not accustomed to the heat in Dubai.

"No, I must fast," I tell them. "If I were home with my family, I would be fasting with them." At this, they agree to let me fast, and my uncle tells me that I will be starting a regular work schedule in the shop. I am pleased to hear that. We go out for morning prayer at the mosque and then return home to sleep.

Even though I am tired, I still struggle with sleeping in a bed. And, it happened again! I fell out of bed, but at least this time I did not wake anyone up. I climb back into bed and finally fall asleep. The next time I wake up, I see it is two o'clock in the afternoon! My uncle and Wali Jan are not at home, so I get cleaned up and dressed, and walk to the shop by myself. In the heat of the day, I get extremely thirsty. The shop feels as hot as fire, but I cannot have anything to eat or drink—not even water—until the evening call for prayer. I wonder if I can last until evening without drinking any water. But I do. And so, every day for a month, I keep up my fasting during the day and fill up on water and food in the evening.

* * *

The next day is our religious holiday known as Eid al-Fitr. This day marks the end of Ramadan, and all the community comes together with friends and family to celebrate. I know how my Baba and Mom will celebrate Eid at home, but I don't know how the people of Dubai will celebrate it. I miss home and wish I were there with my family. I am not getting accustomed to life here, and certainly not my bed!

In preparing for Eid, we close the shop early. When I get back home, I see that my uncle has bought new clothes for me—even new shoes! I am so thankful to my uncle for buying me all these new things.

"Uncle, how many days will the shop be closed to celebrate Eid?"

"Only two days, Hayat," he responds. "When working here, there are only two days of the year that the shop is closed and you won't have to work."

I laugh, because I think he is joking, but my uncle actually speaks the truth. Our only two days off work are during Eid.

In the morning, we go to the mosque early for the Eid prayer. After that, we return home and I am excited because I get to call my family in Afghanistan on this special day. I speak with Baba and tell him about everything I have been doing. He tells me I also need to talk to Mom. Yes, of course! But when I hear my mom's voice on the phone, I get overwhelmed and start to cry, and I can't stop. Mom asks me if I got new clothes for Eid, and I tell her everything Uncle Ibrahim has bought for me.

"What about Juma? How is Juma?" I ask.

"Juma comes to our house every day to ask if we have heard from you. We tell him we have not yet received any calls from you, but if he comes today, Hayat, I will be certain to have him call you." I can't stop crying when I think about how much I miss Juma.

Then I ask Mom if I can speak to my baby brother. Mom says yes and she helps Sadiqullah talk to me on the phone. He is very sweet and cute as he talks to me. Then I hear Mom say that someone is knocking at the door. She takes the phone from Sadiqullah and tells me to wait while she goes to see who is at the door. I hope in my heart that it is Juma who has gone to visit them. Then I hear his voice and the next thing I know we are talking on the phone! I tell him as much as I can about everything I have been doing since my arrival in Dubai. Juma tells me to talk to his brother about getting him a visa. I tell him I will do that—as soon as Eid is over.

"I visit Eid Muhammad in his shop whenever I can, Juma, and I will ask him to work on getting a visa for you."

I am on the phone with my family and Juma for a long time. I feel much better and happier after having spoken with everyone. When my call ends, we sit down to eat breakfast, and my uncle tells me that afterwards we will catch a taxi and go to Creek Park.

In the taxi, Wali Jan and I talk about the differences between how Eid is celebrated in Afghanistan and how we are celebrating it in Dubai. The differences are huge. And even though Dubai has many nice parks and playgrounds, I miss the natural jungle where Juma and I used to play. People from all different countries stroll around Creek Park. Wali Jan suggests we go to the PlayStation theme park. I am amazed at all the technology around us, and we spend several hours there, having lots of fun. We return home that evening and have dinner earlier than usual. We are all tired, so we go to bed right after dinner.

The next day, we are still off work for the Eid celebration. Our plans for the day include going to the Jumeirah Open Beach after breakfast and later to a live concert of some Afghan singers who are visiting Dubai. Wali Jan and I go to the beach together. This quickly becomes one of my favorite places in Dubai. We stay there until evening, after which we go to Bur Dubai, a historic area in the city, to see the live concert of a popular Afghan singer Bahram Jan. I have only listened to his music on cassette tapes before, so to see him at a live concert is amazing.

When we arrive at the club where the concert is to take place, we see a lot of people who are waiting in line to buy their tickets to get into the concert. I think there might be too many for us to get in, but we are eventually able to get tickets. I have never seen anything like this, as I have never attended a concert before. The concert lasts until midnight, after which we return home. Wali Jan says he is hungry and asks me if I want anything to eat. I tell him no, that I am too tired and just want to go to bed.

When I wake up the next morning, I remind myself that Eid is over and it is time to go to the shop to work. And this becomes my routine now for the rest of my life. Every six months, my uncle goes to Afghanistan and my Baba comes to Dubai. Six months later, they switch again. My uncle always goes shopping for his trip back to Afghanistan. He usually starts shopping months before he returns. He buys modern, updated technology items and phones for the family and new clothes and dresses for the women. He usually buys socks and shoes; linens and blankets; and gold jewelry, makeup, shampoo, and personal hygiene items for the women. I also help him get ready. That evening, he brings home everything he bought and I help him pack. Uncle Ibrahim leaves for Afghanistan the next night, but he must travel there via Pakistan, as he has a Pakistani passport. He and Baba, even though they are both Afghani, have Pakistani passports from having lived in refugee camps in Pakistan during the Soviet-Afghan war. In fact, many Afghani citizens do not have passports from their home country.

The next morning, I do not go to the shop because my uncle is leaving. I have been in Dubai for less than one year of my life, and that day I will have neither my uncle nor my Baba next to me. I am frightened and sad beyond belief at the thought of being without any close member of my family nearby. But I ride with my uncle to the airport where we say goodbye, and I return home afterwards. I think about Baba and how he will be here in a few days. I cannot wait to see him.

In the time before Baba arrives in Dubai, I continue my work at the shop every day. I have learned a little bit of the Arabic language, which has been helpful. One day, on my walk to the shop, I call Baba, but he does not answer the phone. I am sad that I cannot reach him. But then my phone rings and I see he is calling me right back. I ask him about Uncle Ibrahim and Baba tells me he made it to Afghanistan without any problem and that he is fine. At that moment, I feel very alone.

"Baba, when are you coming to Dubai?" I ask.

"I leave the day after tomorrow."

I'm happy to hear that, but I tell him I will call him again the next day.

"That is fine, Hayat. You can call me tomorrow."

Our conversation has ended by the time I reach the shop, and I am very happy thinking about my Baba coming to Dubai.

Two days later, I call Baba. He answers my call, but he sounds unhappy to be leaving home and my little brothers. He knows, however, it is time for him to leave, as he has spent more time at home than usual. I know how Baba is feeling, because I know how sad it is to leave our family and our country.

"Hayat, I will arrive in Dubai in three days because I must travel via Pakistan."

I am sad because I wish he were arriving in one day instead of three, but now I will have to wait.

Three days later, Baba calls me from the international airport in Karachi, Pakistan, to tell me he will be arriving in Dubai in two hours! I am so happy to hear that news. I get ready and go to the airport to meet my Baba.

At the airport, I wait for Baba inside Terminal 1. When he comes through the doors, I just hug him and hold onto him for a long time. I am so happy to see my father.

On our way home, he says, "Hayat, you are grown up!"

"How can I be grown up in just a few months, my Baba?" I ask.

But Baba is serious. In Dubai, people grow up very fast. The fast-paced cosmopolitan way of life has people working long hours with only one holiday a year when shops close. I don't know how this is, but maybe because everyone is very comfortable in Dubai and they think the lifestyle is less stressful.

Back at the house, I leave Baba to unpack while I go to a restaurant to pick up lunch for both Baba and me. When we sit down to eat, I ask Baba about Mom and my sisters and my baby brothers. I ask him repeatedly about Juma, too.

"Everyone is fine, Hayat," my father reassures me.

We finish eating and I tell Baba to get some rest. I want to ask him about the Taliban, but I choose to say nothing for now.

Baba goes to sleep and I go to the shop. That night, I close the shop myself and walk home alone. Our routine between home and the shop continues like this for several days. Then, Baba surprises me when he says I should join some language classes.

"Hayat, I know you want to learn English and Arabic properly, so I think you should sign up for classes."

The very next day I sign up for English and Arabic classes at the Supreme Computer Training Center. They teach both languages and computer lessons, but I signed up for only the language classes. I paid to take two languages for one month. I will attend two daily classes, one for each language. And so, I am once again back in a classroom and happy to be learning. My life goes on like this for some time. The next day is December 31 and the teachers tell me there will be no classes for two days.

Chapter Eleven
2010

I love being in school again, but now have two days off. I ask Baba about New Year's Eve and New Year's Day, which I have never celebrated before and know nothing about. "What happens on these days? What do people do?"

"Well, Hayat, people are off work, so they go to the park or to the beach. Many people also have a party to celebrate."

"Oh. So people celebrate a new year?"

"Yes."

Now I understand why my teacher told me classes were canceled for two days! It's a holiday, and another new experience for me.

Wali Jan and I go to Jumeirah to celebrate New Year's Eve. We walk through crowded streets and see that everyone is waiting for midnight. When the new year arrives, people are spraying each other with water pistols and tossing water balloons. We have a lot of fun, and finally return home by 4:00 a.m. I go to sleep and the rest of New Year's Day is quiet for us. The next morning comes quickly and it is once again time to open the shop and get back to work.

On January 4, the city of Dubai celebrates the official opening of Burj Dubai, the tallest tower in the world. The tower, known today as Burj Khalifa, stands at 829.8 meters (2,722 feet) and is located in the heart of Dubai's business district.

On the night of the official opening, the city holds fireworks to celebrate. I have never seen fireworks before and am looking forward to this experience. Baba, Wali Jan, and I go downtown where the celebration is to occur. But there are a lot of people and traffic, so we are unable to get up close to the Burj Dubai building. We find a place to sit farther away and watch the fireworks. At first, they remind me of the helicopters back home that shine their big light down to the ground in a single flash. Dubai's fireworks are much larger and more colorful, however. When the fireworks show is over, we return home.

The next morning, I get ready to go to work in the shop. Later in the day I go to my language classes. And my life continues on like this week after week. By August, I have completed my language classes, and I can speak and write English and Arabic well.

In a few days, we will enter the fasting month of Ramadan. I'm remembering from the year before the forty-five-degree days that were just too hot to completely fast unless you were in an air-conditioned environment. The manager of our market says we will finally be allowed to move into the new Naif Souq market, and we will be there by the first day of Ramadan. Everyone is happy to hear this news, because this market has air conditioning and also because it is a very famous place for shopping.

August 11 is the day all the shopkeepers and traders in our temporary market are given the approval to move into Naif Market. Our shop, number 007, is located on the outside of the building, on the main round opposite the entrance to Al Manal Centre, which is another large shopping center. Baba and I pack and ship all our goods to our new shop. By the first day of Ramadan, we have finished moving everything. At last! We have air conditioning and I now feel much more comfortable about fasting. I am able to continue my observance of this tradition the entire month.

With just one day left before Ramadan ends and we have the Eid celebration, I call home and speak with my Uncle Ibrahim. I give him all the updates on how Baba and I moved our shop to the new location at Naif Souq market. When we finish talking, I ask to speak to Mom. I find that every time I call home, speaking with Mom gets easier. Even though I really miss her, I always make sure to tell her I'm happy here—mostly because I want her to be happy. I also get to speak with my sisters and brothers, and really enjoy hearing their voices.

"Mom, I will call you back another time soon. For now, I must go. Tomorrow is Eid and I have to pick up my new outfit from the tailors." After we end our call, I close the shop for the day. On my way home, I stop at the tailor and pick up my Eid clothes.

In the morning, Baba, Wali Jan, and I go to the mosque for Eid prayers. After that, we return home for breakfast and make our plans for the day's outing.

"Today, Hayat," Baba says, "I would like to take you to the Al Ain mountains."

We agree and take a three-hour taxi ride to the mountains, where we spend the entire day. I realize I have not been on a long drive since leaving Afghanistan. But the roads in Afghanistan aren't really roads—they are just rocky paths. The roads here in UAE are like those I have seen in movies—smooth and paved. Among the Al Ain mountains is Jebel Hafeet, a very high mountain that is famous for its natural hot springs. The area is lush with greenery, and air temperatures at Jebel Hafeet are much cooler than in Dubai. I love the natural green, as it reminds me of my jungle back home. After spending a relaxing and refreshing day here, evening falls and it is time to return home.

We get home at midnight, which gives me just enough time to sleep for a few hours before the shops open in the morning. Some shops remain closed for a second day of Eid celebration, but I decided to open my shop at 8 a.m. In fact, that becomes my routine. I open the shop every morning at eight, and remain open until 11:30 at night. My workdays are long, but I don't get tired easily and I am happy to be working.

On October 20, the Dubai municipality will officially open the Naif Souq market, even though we had our soft opening on the first day of Ramadan. Before the original Naif Souq burned down, it housed nearly two hundred shops. We now enjoy a newly constructed market with entrances on all four sides and central air conditioning. Two hundred eighteen shops occupy space in the souq: 111 on the ground floor and 107 on the first floor. In addition, there are forty-four kiosks, two escalators, and two elevators. The center is equipped with modern amenities such as rest rooms, parking lots, coffee shops, and municipal offices. The basement parking lot can accommodate up to 99 vehicles. The building houses three coffee shops on the ground floor as well as two offices on the first floor, one on the ground floor, and one in the basement level.

After the blaze gutted the old building, the municipality distributed compensation to the shop owners who were also exempted from paying any additional rents until the new Naif Souq opened. The municipality also launched a special advertising campaign in different media to promote the new souq in the Gulf countries in order to continue to attract those people who used to visit the old souq. Naif Souq had been one of the oldest traditional markets in Dubai, named for its proximity to the ancient Naif Fort, which had once served as Dubai's police headquarters and prison. The market, originally sixty thousand square feet in size, was also popularly referred to in Arabic as Souq Sanadiq because the shops it contained were box-like before a 1980 renovation occurred.

That day, the shop owners are all happy with the municipality's official opening of Naif Souq, and the fact that people who have never been to the souq will hear the media's announcement of this opening and hopefully come here to shop and make business better for everyone.

Chapter Twelve
2011

Work in the shop continues as it has all along. We work long days and are happy to be in our new location at Naif Souq. One day, Baba tells me he plans to get me a visa so I can travel to China. As fabric traders, we must travel the globe to buy fabrics wholesale, and China is well known for its huge textile fairs.

"I want you to go to China, Hayat, so you can buy fabrics for our shop." I have no interest in going to China. I would rather stay in Dubai where I can just work in our shop and stay near our village friends who also own shops. Baba has always been the one to travel to China, and I want him to continue making those trips. In the end, I agree with Baba's plan.

I go home to retrieve my passport. At home, I look everywhere I can think of for my passport, but I have no idea where it is. I call Wali Jan to see if he knows where my passport might be, but he doesn't know either. I return to the shop to tell Baba I have lost my passport. I am really scared to tell him. Baba isn't the kind of person who angers easily, but this is a big problem. Even I couldn't believe I lost my passport. Losing your passport in Dubai stops your life because inside the passport is your residency visa.

When I tell Baba I am unable to find my passport, he remains quiet. But his quiet speaks a thousand words. I can almost hear his voice reminding me that I need to always keep my identification with me. "Let's go," he tells me, and together we go to the Naif Police Station, which is the closest police station to our market. The police tell me to write a letter of complaint. I do as I am told, but the police now tell me I must take the letter to the Consulate General of Afghanistan in Dubai. When I arrive at the consulate, I show them my letter, and they tell me I must have it signed by the court in Dubai and also by the Ministry of Foreign Affairs of Dubai. And off I go in taxi to both of these places. I tell myself I will never lose my passport again! By day's end, I complete everything I've been told I need to do. Tomorrow I will return to the consulate to get a new passport.

I arrive at the consulate first thing in the morning, where I show them my letter and provide the two necessary photos. They tell me to return at two in the afternoon to pick up my new passport.

By 2:00 p.m., I am back at the consulate and my new passport is ready. Now I have to have my Dubai visa added to my passport, and that can take up to five days. I leave my passport at an official government-approved typing center, where they will handle all the work.

The next day, Juma's brother Eid stops by my shop. He tells me he wants Juma to come to Dubai and shows me Juma's passport. I just cannot believe this news I am hearing! I'm so happy Juma will finally be coming to Dubai. Eid tells me Juma will have his visa in about two weeks.

After five days, I return to the typing center to inquire about my passport and visa. They tell me it is ready, so I pay them the typing money and once again feel secure now that I have my new passport.

The next day I go to a travel agency to request a business visa to be able to travel to China. The easiest visa to get in Dubai is a visa for China. We can get one at any travel agency. At the travel agency, they tell me the timeframe to obtain the visa is ten days and the total cost for the visa is two thousand Dirhams, with one thousand Dirhams to be paid in advance. I pay the money, leave them my passport, and return to my shop. I decide to stop in and see Juma's brother to find out how Juma's visa is coming along.

"Juma's visa has been rejected three times, Hayat," Eid says. I am so disappointed to hear this news. "But I will speak with his sponsor to see if we can get help on this matter." There is nothing I can do but wait.

In ten days, I go back to the travel agency to inquire about my visa. They tell me it is ready, so I pay them the remaining balance of the money owed. Back at our shop, I show my father my new visa and he is happy to know everything is resolved.

"Very good, Hayat. Go and buy your airplane ticket to leave the day after tomorrow."

I have secured my ticket to leave for China in two days. Baba wants to accompany me to the airport, but I tell him there is no need and that I can go alone. "I'm fine, Baba," I tell him, and so he lets me go alone.

I take the thirty-minute taxi ride to Terminal Three, which is one of the largest at the Dubai airport. Inside, I go into the Immigrations area and wait. While there, I see an Indian man I recognize as a shopper in our market. He tells me that he, too, is traveling to China. I ask him all about China, and he tells me there is nothing to worry about when traveling to China. We get through Immigrations, and I am now onboard the plane. As the plane takes off, I think about how this is only my second time flying.

After a very long flight—nearly nine hours—we finally arrive in China. We leave the airport and take a taxi to the Shanghai Hotel. I check into my room and then go down to the hotel's market to buy some food. For me, the food must be halal. I realize most hotels don't cook halal food, and I'm not certain about other foods I see. In the end, I decide to eat fruit, so I buy enough to last me for a day or two.

In the morning, I go to the fabric market in Guangzhou, which is home to Guangzhou International Textile City, one of the largest textile procurement places in Asia. Baba's plan is for me to remain in China for one month, but I finish buying what I need in seven days. I really just want to leave China and return to Dubai, as I do not like any part of that country. As I ride the taxi back to the airport for my return flight, I think about how good it will be to be back in Dubai—even after the long flight.

When we land in Dubai, the first thing I do is go to a restaurant in the airport. I am hungry, as I did not eat any real food in China for seven days other than fruit. I lost two kilos in seven days! But I now enjoy a meal of food I know I can eat, and take a taxi home from there. The trip has been tiring, so I go right to bed.

That night, Baba comes home from the shop and sees that I am home. "Hayat, did you buy anything in China or did you just come back without buying anything?" he asks.

"Baba, I bought many fabrics and provided the shipping company all the information they need. Everything will arrive here in eighteen to twenty-four days."

"Why did you not stay in China the entire month as we planned?"

I tell him about my difficulty finding halal food, and that I'd been eating only fruit for the previous week. Baba laughs at me and tells me I should have asked someone to help me find halal restaurants. "Now you know what to do the next time you go."

I say nothing in response, but instead think, "I am never going back there, Baba."

* * *

After being away from the shop for ten days, I look forward to getting back to work. On my first day back, Juma's brother appears in our shop.

"Hayat, would you like to come to the airport with me to pick up Juma?" Eid asks.

What can I say! I can't believe I am finally going to see my best friend after so many months. At the airport, we wait outside for Juma, just as my uncle waited for me so long ago. When he finally exits the airport, I cannot believe my eyes. He is all grown up. "Now you are a complete man, Juma!" And he says the same thing about me.

I go with Juma to his brother's house where we have dinner together. After that, I go back home. I cannot stop thinking about how happy I am to finally have Juma with me in Dubai. I can't remember a time in life when Juma and I were not together.

* * *

The fabrics I purchased in China finally arrive. I sell everything in just nine days and make a huge profit on the entire deal.

"Hayat," Baba says, "you must go back to China for more."

"Baba, I don't think I need to go back to China. Why don't we use the money we just made and grow our business? We could buy another shop."

Baba thinks for just a moment. "I agree with your idea. Now, walk through the market and find us another good shop to buy."

I look through the entire market, upstairs and down, and find two shops available inside on the second floor, and one shop available outside. I choose the outside shop for good reason, and it also happens to be very close to Juma's brother's shop. His shop is number 15 and the one we intend to buy is number 18. I speak with the owner of shop number 18, and he is ready to sell the shop immediately. He tells me the price is one million Dirhams. We have 800,000 Dirhams in cash now, so the shop owner agrees to this price. He asks for half the money now and the remainder at the end of the year.

At the conclusion of this business deal, Baba says he must return to Afghanistan, where he will remain for up to two years. And Uncle Ibrahim will, of course, return to Dubai. I am comforted knowing that I am right next to Juma every day. We see each other and talk just like we did growing up in our own country.

Chapter Thirteen
2012

One day, two women come to the Naif Souq—a white woman and a young black woman. I think the black girl, who is about twenty-five years old, is the white woman's maid or assistant, but it turns out she is the woman's daughter. I am confused by this, naturally. But I recognize the black girl. She has bought fabric from me in the past, and I know she likes to negotiate a low price.

I learn their names are Leslie and Zeinab. To be exact, they tell me they are Leslie Putnam Orr and Zeineba Nurhassen Oumer. Zeinab is really funny. She calls Leslie "Leslie Putnam Orr" when she is trying to get Leslie to pay attention to something she wants to say. Leslie gets distracted easily by talking to anyone and everyone. Interestingly, she isn't bothered that she speaks only English and usually has no idea what people are saying to her.

Leslie is very friendly, but I find her behavior to be funny, or "ridiculous," which is a word she taught me. She says "ridiculous" all the time. That, and also "I love it!" American movies taught me two sayings that always remind me of my friendship with Leslie, "Fasten your seat belt" and "love-hate relationship." At first I think Leslie will be like the American soldiers I met at home in Afghanistan, but she is not. She loves to talk about everything.

I don't really know what is so exciting about my fabric shop, but Leslie cannot stop buying fabrics that day. I soon learn one more thing about her when she says, "Hayat, I don't have any money with me today to pay for all this fabric." But then she leaves the shop with bags overflowing with my fabric.

Zeinab tells me Leslie is sick from something that happened to her in Africa, and that she will be going back to America. When Leslie was about to leave the shop that first day I meet her, I ask her if she ever used WhatsApp messenger service.

"Yes!" she replies. Then, characteristically, she adds, "I love it!"

She leaves for America in December. I think it will be nice to call her on Christmas Day. When I do, her father answers, and gets very angry with me. It turns out, my call was actually at night. I had forgotten about the nine-hour time difference.

To this day, Leslie and I remain the best of friends. She tells me I am good looking and have an unbelievable smile. And though we have our moments of heated discussion on a variety of topics, we are just as quickly once again best friends and enjoy much laughter together. In all honesty, I am friends with her because she is so open and friendly—and when we first met, she did not judge me as a person who spoke very little English.

Chapter Fourteen
2013

This year, things are changing quite a bit for me. I go home to Afghanistan, where I remain for four months. Leslie moves back to the UAE, but this time she is in Abu Dhabi, and we continue to communicate via WhatsApp on our cell phones.

At the end of Ramadan, I go to spend Eid with Leslie in Abu Dhabi. I take a cousin along with me for the visit. When we get into the elevator with Leslie to go up to her home, she tells me to press the button for the fifth floor. I tell her that I am the guest and that she should push the button herself.

Leslie's friend Muhammad brings us biryani, an Indian mixed rice dish, but I refuse to eat that. In fact, I refuse to eat anything. As does my cousin, who does not speak English. When Leslie offers us strawberries, we do not eat them either because she has removed the green stems and they are from Pakistan.

Leslie gets very annoyed with me. In fact, I am so rude that day, I make her cry. I learn from her later that she was uncomfortable having my cousin and me in her western home. I am certain she was happy to see us leave. After that, she does not call me for a very long time. Up until Ramadan, Leslie had been visiting me in Dubai every Friday for early breakfast. But now she stops visiting me as much as she used to.

Leslie does, however, one thing that makes me really happy. She remembers from when we first met that I am frustrated with English adverbs and that I wished I knew them all. She then took the time to make me a book of adverbs and have it printed for me. The book contains many chapters, all with good examples.

I am fortunate in that I can speak four languages: English, Arab, Urdu, and some Hindi. At the Naif Souk, many of the shopkeepers, including Baba, speak only Pashto and just a little English. When they need help, they come to me, and I am always happy when I am able to help them.

Chapter Fifteen
2014

Time flies by quickly. Baba left Dubai at the end of 2011 and returned early this year. Now it is time for me to go back to Afghanistan. Baba, Wali Jan, and I rotate going back and forth between our home and family in Paktika province and our business in Dubai. Just a few days remain before the start of the Ramadan festival, and I ask Baba if I can go to Afghanistan at that time for vacation. Baba says yes.

So now I am planning to go back to Afghanistan. It is a long time for me to not see my mother or my family. I am so excited at the thought of going home, tears come to my eyes. I call Leslie to let her know this news, but I know she never answers my call the first time. Most times, I must call her two or three times. She always answers my call after I call a third time, and she is always angry. I can be certain she will always say, "Why do you call so many times?" At that, I ask her why she has to be a red hot chili pepper, and that makes her even angrier. I have fun teasing her like this.

This call is different, however. When she finally answers the phone, I speak before she can say anything, mostly to save myself from one of her lectures about calling too many times.

"I am going back to Afghanistan after five years of being away."

"Oh, Hayat, I am so happy for you. I will come to see you before you leave for Afghanistan, okay?'

"Yes, absolutely."

Now I decide I need to go shopping for gifts for my family. I buy gifts for my sisters and brothers, and especially for Mom and my niece. My sister Sobia now has a daughter, Robina, who is already two years old. I cannot believe I have never seen her, except in pictures. She looks very cute, from what I can tell in the photos.

This year, Ramadan starts in June, and only a few days remain before it starts. I have finished all my shopping and that night Leslie visits. We go out for dinner to my favorite Afghan kabob restaurant in Dubai. Their food is delicious. Leslie tells me how happy she is for me.

"I am very happy too," I tell her. "I can't wait to get back to Afghanistan."

After dinner, Leslie heads home, as do I. In the morning, I must buy my airplane ticket for my trip.

My flight leaves at midnight the following day, and I decide not to go to my shop that day. I have a new salesman who, with Baba, will take care of the shop while I am gone. I spend the day at home, mostly waiting for night to arrive so I can fly back home to my motherland Afghanistan.

Juma accompanies me to the airport. He would have liked to have come home with me, but his brother is in China, so he cannot leave at this time. When Ramadan ends, Juma will be able to come to Afghanistan.

I tell him, "Juma, please, *please*, call your brother to come back to Dubai quickly so you can spend your vacation in Afghanistan while I am there. Juma says he will call his brother in the morning, but we are no longer the little boys we once were. We are now grown and we even shave. But when I talk with Juma, it still feels to me as though we are little kids. The time has come for me to go into the Immigration area at the airport, so I say my goodbye to Juma.

I get through Immigration without any problem and am now on the plane. I take some pictures looking down over Dubai once the plane is in the air. The city looks amazing at night. Exactly two and a half hours later we approach Kabul International Airport, and I can't believe that the city below is Kabul. It looks so big! I see beautiful lights below as I look down from the airplane window.

When I get off the plane, I stand on the nearby ground and the cool breeze of Kabul brings tears to my eyes. I was still a boy when I left Afghanistan, but now I'm returning a man. I am unable to control myself, and I get down on my knees and kiss the ground. People all around me watch and ask how long I'd been gone and where I came from.

"I am returning to my motherland after being away for five years."

I catch a taxi outside the airport and ask the driver to take me to a good hotel in Kabul. The driver tells me the good hotels are in an area of Kabul known as Wazir Akbar Khan.

"Take me there," I tell him.

We come to the Wazir Akbar Khan Mustafa Hotel first. This is where I decide to book my room for the night. I notice that Kabul is now completely changed. For example, women are working at the hotel reception desk. I still find it hard to believe that this is Kabul, as changed as it is. That night I rest well at the hotel, as I want to get an early start on my trip to Paktika Province.

I awake at sunrise, shower, put on clean clothes, and leave the hotel. I rent a car and drive from Kabul to Ghazni Province. In Ghazni, I get a different rental car and drive to our district in Paktika Province.

The road is no longer the way it was five years earlier, that is, covered in stone. I think I'm still in Dubai, as the road is now paved and smooth. On my drive home, I see how everything has changed. When I reach Paktika Province, I almost think again that I am still in Kabul. How fast everything has been built up.

After the long drive home, I see Mom waiting for me at the door as I approach. I remember my first day of school when she was waiting for me at the door. I am unable to control myself and I start crying. I turn my head to hide my tears from my mother, but she says, "You are still for me my little Hayat. Come, give me a hug. Don't hide your tears."

I get out of the car and run to her. At first, she is smiling as we hug, but when I pull away and look into her eyes I see she, too, is crying.

"Mom, when I first hugged you, you were smiling. Now you have tears in your eyes too?"

"Hayat, I smile because I am seeing my son after five years. But the tears come out because you were very young when you left for Dubai. You were hugging my legs. But now I look at you and see you are all grown up and even taller than me."

We go inside together. My sisters are waiting for me and everyone gives me hugs. I'm so happy to see them all. My two little brothers Sadiqullah and Najeebullah have also grown. Next I ask my mom to make me lunch because I really missed the lunches she used to make me. She agrees and is now cooking lunch.

"Sobia, where is your daughter Robina?" I ask my oldest sister.

Sobia tells me Robina is with her father and that maybe they will come later.

Lunch is finally ready and I sit down to eat. Actually, it is not even lunchtime, but I just missed my mom's lunch so much.

My mute Uncle Marjan comes home from the village. Mom and my sisters tell me to wait to see if he even remembers me. I don't think he'll recognize that this is me, Hayat, because I'm now a man. But when Marjan enters the room, he looks at me and runs right over to give me a hug. He places his hands on my shoulders. When I look at him, I see tears in his eyes. He wipes away his tears. Marjan looks at my mother and uses his hands to signal that he recognizes me as Hayat. We are all very happy.

I am very tired that night. I missed sleeping on the floor, but I need to ask my mom which is my room because they knocked down the old rooms and rebuilt a new house on the same land. Mom shows me my room. It is beautiful! I go into my room and fall right to sleep.

When I wake up in the morning, I go out to the main room where my family is waiting. I give everyone their gifts. Even my little niece Robina is here with Akal Khan. I give her the dresses and toys I bought for her in Dubai. When we are done with the gifts, Mom brings me breakfast.

"Mom, after breakfast I need to go see my teacher Naseeb Khan." When I am finished eating, I drive to my former teacher's house. I knock on the door and it is opened by a little boy, Naseeb's six-year-old son. He tells me to go inside. Before entering, I ask if Naseeb Khan is at home. The boy tells me, "Baba hasn't moved for the last six months."

"Why?" I ask. "What happened?"

"He has only one leg now. The doctor cut off his other leg," the boy says.

Then I hear another voice from inside—the voice of my teacher. "Who is there? Who are you speaking to?"

I step inside their house and go to the room where my teacher is sitting. He looks at me as though he recognizes me, but he is a bit unsure. "Is this Hayat?"

I see his leg and tears come to my eyes. "Yes, sir," I say, the same as always.

My teacher is now crying, and through his tears he says, "I have not been to school for the past six months. I have not been able to prove to my village students that I'm a good teacher." Teaching has been Naseeb's entire world. He believes he can no longer be a good teacher and that his career is over. For Naseeb to believe this is terrible, as he feels teaching is his duty, and he has devoted all of his energy and poured his heart into teaching. He even risked his life by continuing to teach during the time of the Taliban government.

"Sir, you are the light of our village. You are the teacher of all the hard times we endured."

Naseeb Khan asks his little son to bring us tea. I sit and drink green tea with my teacher. I am upset about what has happened to his leg, and wonder why such difficult things always seem to happen to good people. He explains that in three months he'll be able to use a prosthetic leg and shortly after that he'll be walking again.

He has not yet left his teaching job because I can see he is still reading his students' exam papers. I tell him he is one of the best teachers I ever had, which brings a smile to his face. We visit for a while longer and at noon I leave, although I am sad for him. He understands that I want to be home with my family, since I have not seen them in such a long time. Back at home, I tell my mother about Naseeb Khan, and she is saddened by the news.

Ramadan begins in one day, so we now prepare for the month of fasting that is to come. Five days into Ramadan, my little brothers ask me to take them to the Urgun district so they can order new clothes be made for them for the Eid celebration to come. I agree, and together we go to the Urgun district. I leave my brothers' clothes with the tailor, who will sew them new outfits for Eid. We pick up a few more things for home and then return.

We continue our routine of fasting, and are now into day eighteen of Ramadan. Only twelve days of fasting remain until the Eid, so people everywhere are going out shopping to prepare for this festival. That morning, I drive back to the Urgun district to pick up my brothers' new clothes from the tailor. After I do that, I decide to fill the car with petrol at a nearby station. The time is about ten o'clock. As I am filling my car, I hear a very loud bomb noise from inside the Urgun market. The glass at the petrol station shatters, and I run to the market. Everyone is running toward the market.

"What happened?" I ask.

"A suicide attack by a car inside the market."

I go to the area where the explosion occurred. I see dead bodies and injured people all around me. My mind is not working. I'm confused and don't know what to do. I turn and see an injured child in a car nearby. He's crying and his father's head is resting against the steering wheel. The man is dead. I run to the car and try to open the door, but I can't. I yell for help, and others come to help rescue the little boy from the car. Afghan police are coming with an ambulance behind them, so we hand off the child.

The crying of that little boy remains stuck in my head. This is hell on earth. A river of blood runs everywhere, with eighty-nine dead bodies all around—at least that is what I can see with my own eyes. The Afghan police remove the bodies, but may more are injured or still missing.

I feel myself getting dizzy and fall to the ground. When I open my eyes again I am in the hospital. I tell the doctor there that I am fine. "I'm not injured. I was just dizzy for a moment, but now I'm fine." The doctor allows me to leave the hospital. My car is still parked at the petrol station. I retrieve the car and drive back home. I can still hear the crying of that child who was stuck in the car with his dead father. The image makes me cry all the way home.

Back at home, my mother asks me where I've been. She tried to call me thirty-one times, but I never heard my phone. When she sees me, she asks, "Were you injured in the bomb blast?"

I did not tell her anything about the bomb blast because I did not want her to know about it. But we now have a TV at home, and she tells me she heard about the explosion on TV. Till that moment, I was unaware we had a TV at home. Mom tells me Uncle Ibrahim bought it.

I go inside the house. "I'm fine, Mom," I tell her.

But she looks into my eyes and sees they are red. She forces me to tell her the whole story. She cries upon hearing what happened, but I tell her to not say a thing to anyone. I'm so thirsty, but cannot drink because I am fasting. More than that, I wish I hadn't seen the bomb blast. The image of the child is stuck in my mind and I still hear him crying. The news on TV that night says 129 people were killed and more than 140 injured.

I do not leave our house for five days. Mom tells me I should go to the doctor. I agree. The drive to the doctor's office takes me past the cemetery where I see two new graves. I wonder who else has died, because I had not heard of anyone from our village dying. I stop the car near the new graves and get out. An eight-year-old boy is sitting between the two graves.

"What is your name?" I ask.

"Merwais," the boy responds.

"Who are these graves for?"

"My parents. They were killed in the Urgun bomb blast."

Hearing this, tears come to my eyes. I extend my hand to the boy and say, "Merwais, come. Let's go to the market. I will get you your new clothes for Eid."

The boy is crying as he responds, "No. This was my world, and it has been destroyed. This was my happiness, and it is all gone." As young as this boy is, his words strike me at my heart.

I try again to get him to come with me, but he does not listen to me, insisting he will stay by his parents' graves. I walk back to my car. I next hear the boy running up behind me. I turn and wait for him. When Merwais reaches me, he hands me a business card he has for a tailor's shop.

"My father gave me this card. It's for the tailor who got the order to make my Eid clothes. I see every grave here has a flag on it, but I don't have flags to put on my parents' graves. So, please, ask the tailor to sew two flags from the fabric he was to use for my Eid outfit. Since I don't have my parents with me, I don't want to celebrate Eid."

I hear these words and barely have the energy to speak. I nod and answer simply, "Okay." I hold Merwais in a long hug, and he finally agrees to come home with me. We get in the car and drive away. At home, I introduce him to my brothers and my mother. He is now a part of our family. He is now my brother.

I head out again to first go to the doctor's and then to buy Merwais' Eid clothes and also to fulfill his wish to have two flags made. I finish all these errands and then return home. Mom has changed Merwais into Sadiqullah's clothes, and he looks good. I am so happy to see the kindness my mother is showing Merwais. But I feel the need to say something more to my family. "Everyone needs to treat Merwais as though he is one of us, as though he was born into this family and he is our brother. I just want this little boy to start his new life with a new family."

I ask Mom to call my brothers to my room. I immediately see Sadiqullah, Najeebullah, and Merwais all standing in front of me. I present Merwais with his new Eid clothes and shoes. At first, he smiles when he sees the new outfit, but then gets very serious.

"Did you make the flags?"

My eyes fill with tears once again. I tell him I will figure this out right now. "You stay here and play with your new brothers." Merwais is very smart. I know he needs to see the flags on his parents' graves before he'll be able to settle in with my family.

I tell my mom about the flags, and show her that I had them made for Merwais. Together, Mom, Merwais, and I go back to his parents' gravesite and place the flags on each of the two graves.

"Merwais," my mom says, "you can let your parents rest comfortably. Tell them you have a new family with three brothers and three sisters, and tell them you are being taken care of."

Merwais turns and talks to the two graves. I am unable to control my emotions and go wait in the car. After a few minutes, Mom and Merwais join me. We return home, where Merwais starts his new life with his new family.

It is now the day before Eid. I tell Merwais we should go to the market to do some shopping. He agrees and we head to the market together. My real plan is to buy him school supplies. I want him to be educated. I did a lot of shopping for Merwais, including toys and a ball and bat to play cricket, which I know he loves. We return home and spend the rest of the day preparing for the holiday. In the morning, we go to the homes of our neighbors and family and wish everyone a happy Eid.

After the Eid celebrations end, I take Merwais to enroll him in school. He now studies with my brothers, and I see how he is happier day by day in his new life with my family.

I remain in Afghanistan for four months, after which I return to my business in Dubai. And so the cycle continues.

www.ingramcontent.com/pod-product-compliance
Lightning Source LLC
Chambersburg PA
CBHW070624300426
44113CB00010B/1643